PRAISE FOR IN IN DEMAND B.O.S.S. AND LYNDI MACRAE

The single biggest lesson I've learned as a small business owner, and automation practitioner, is the value of having a clearly defined and intentionally crafted customer journey, and in this book Lyndi masterfully walks you through the key ingredients it takes for any business to design and implement this. Lyndi has a wealth of experience, but her real super power lies in helping take complex topics, and make them less intimidating and more accessible. Anyone who spends time with Lyndi, in person or through this book, can't help but leave feeling more capable and confident in themselves.

Greg Jenkins
Keap Academy Contributor, Founder of Monkeypod Marketing

Lyndi Is A True Student Of Her Craft

I've watched Lyndi grow from an automation beginner to a true master of relationships at scale. Any time our paths cross it's always a delight. She understands that automation is a tool to engender a tribe around a certain brand/offer. She is 100% a BOSS!

Paul Sokol - 3.14th Master Automation Jedi From The 10's (https://www.paulsokol.me)

"Lyndi MacRae has a superior knack for solving big business problems with automation. As a small business growth expert and Keap coach, Lyndi simplifies complex ideas and creates clarity for entrepreneurs who struggle to get organized so they can grow and scale. Learn from one of the best --GET THIS BOOK.

-Carmen Campbell, Director, Customer Onboarding at Keap

—--

"At last a book that demystifies automatic systems. Lyndi shares her passion and shows us how to leverage our time and get more done with less effort.

In pure dollar terms, this book is the step-by-step guide to maximising the profit potential of every new lead you get.

This should be required reading for anyone marketing online."

Pete Godfrey – Wizard of Words
https://www.facebook.com/groups/PeteGodfreyShow

—

As a business consultant the first thing I develop with clients is their database.

Over the last 12 years I have watched Lyndi become a master of using the power of a CRM to grow businesses.

I urge you to listen to everything Lyndi teaches and employ her strategies. Your business will thank you.

I am more than happy to endorse Lyndi.

PRAISE FOR IN DEMAND B.O.S.S. AND LYNDI MACRAE

Ian Marsh
Streetsmart Business Consultants.
streetsmartbusinessconsultants.com.au

———

'Having worked on hundreds of sales funnels I know that automation is key to reaching more by doing less. Working with Lyndi to have an onboarding foundation setup, training, and ongoing support means that my clients are achieving high ROI from the very first contact point with their potential customers because everything is in place for a seamless customer journey. Having Keap as the CRM means that our potential customers' journey is personalised to their online behaviour, automated, and tracked so we can see the real campaign results from that very first email'

Eve John
Copywriter and Course Creator

———

***

Lyndi explains the backend of business in an engaging and entertaining way. Her book is informative and filled with highly beneficial ideas that can easily be actioned. Whether you are starting out on your entrepreneurial journey or you are a seasoned business owner, Lyndi's expertise is sure to bring a high ROI.

Sophia Marie Lightfoot,

Women's Weight Loss and Body Image Specialist

***

Lyndi creates magic with BOSS. I've worked with Lyndi for many years and have witnessed her growth first hand. She gifted me a solid gold foundation for Simply Better Health C. (Pty Ltd). It's heaven to move forward with systems in place and it's been so much easier to onboard my team into the business too.

On reflection, it was only my procrastination that held me back. Lyndi had my back when I ventured out into the world wide web from being a clinician in a room for 25 years. I'm running courses I have only dreamt about and speaking around the world. Sharing my wisdom and life experience is now creating and supporting my lifestyle.

To have a website is one thing… to get a presence is another. I have written a book and contributed to a few, been interviewed on podcasts, invited to speak at conferences overseas that all gave me a presence. Whilst I shared all the foregoing, it didn't get me the connections I was after. I've learnt that knowing your audience and tailoring keywords appropriately is paramount. I have evergreen blogs that can be recycled for promotional purposes, along with automations that keep my audience engaged, booking in to chat and moving onto being clients.

Every year I become clearer and clearer, coming back to my message to Change the Way the World sees Health - 'Bringing Humanity Back to Nature'. The clearer I am the more confidence I have, which in turn attracts like-minded clients.

The frustration of business not making ends meet, really translated into me being the worlds' best kept secret! Oh the fear of being successful gripped me… what if I start something and can't keep up, let clients down and become overwhelmed, unable to continue what I started? Eeeekkk… what then? Sound familiar?

PRAISE FOR IN DEMAND B.O.S.S. AND LYNDI MACRAE

Not being a techy and glazing over at just the thought, sent me into a myriad of excuses as to why I couldn't tackle these systems myself. Confused and with difficulty in staying present on zoom calls with Lyndi, we decided to begin to do campaigns in Keap, update my website and set up courses in Member Vault on the calls. Voila, it clicked! Now I am able to do much of this myself and understand what my VA's will be handling as I pass tasks over.

Everything Lyndi does is practical, logical, interesting and helpful… It's given me the backbone of my business.

Once I realised I had everything at my fingertips, that clients could book and pay online for consultations, programs and courses… life became oh so much easier.

Today I have clients from all over the world booking in to speak to me, to look at the best way forward to work together.

Sometimes you don't realise what gold you have until you begin to share. Now my business is on autopilot, I have more time to write my books and create more courses and of course spend more time with family and friends.

Would I recommend Lyndi? Absolutely, in a heartbeat! She's the gold member of your team, guiding, teaching and supporting you to build the business of your dreams.

Sandy B Simmons
Founder
Simply Better Health Pty Ltd

———

KEAP and Lyndi have transformed my business

I run a wellness clinic, Happy & Healthy Wellbeing Centre, in the southern Sydney suburb of Miranda. For ever my admin team had managed the hundreds of new enquiries we receive by email and website manually. It was labour intensive and clunky. I was aware of CRMs and had tried a few out like Hubspot but we didn't get much improvement in efficiency because we didn't have the expertise or the time to become experts in using it.

Lyndi who had coached me previously to run groups on Facebook recommended I switch to KEAP. It was a great decision to make the move to KEAP because it has transformed the way we do business.

With Lyndi's expertise all possible manual processes that could be automated have been automated. Incoming enquiries, lead generation, our weekly emails to patients, new patients management and our online programs are now managed with automated within KEAP. The number of things KEAP now does for us has freed up so much time for my admin team to work on higher value tasks. And I know we have only just scratched the surface in what it can do for my business.

Without Lyndi and her team we would have been lost but because of her KEAP expertise our automated processes have been designed and implemented easily and smoothly.

There is no way we can now live without KEAP and Lyndi, they are integral to my businesses management and growth.

Hayden Keys

Naturopath & founder of Happy & Healthy Wellbeing Centre

FOREWORD
for In Demand B.O.S.S.

There's something unique and powerful about the small business space. All around the world it attracts people with vision, with drive, and with a sense of purpose. Among the many things I find inspiring about the global small business community is that no matter how different we, or our businesses, are – time and time again, our challenges are the same.

And trust me, I realize that saying this doesn't immediately resolve the different obstacles you may be facing in your business, but I hope you feel some comfort knowing that you can draw on the wisdom of others who have been where you are going.

In Demand B.O.S.S. is an invaluable example of that type of wisdom. Chapter-by-chapter, Lyndi has distilled her real world experience working behind the scenes to help businesses develop and implement systems into digestible stories and actionable advice specifically to help you shortcut the learning curve that far too many businesses have struggled to surmount. I can't count the number of business lessons I've learned over the years, but among the most important is the value of having a clearly defined and intentionally crafted customer experience. And, good news for you – the specific framework I recommend for doing this successfully is introduced and explored throughout the book you're already holding.

If you have had even one customer, then that customer had a journey. And if your customers have a journey, then it may as

well be one you've intentionally designed and that produces results in a reliable and predictable fashion.

The three pillars of that system are to collect leads, convert them into clients, and then create fans from those clients. While this framework might sound easy, I assure you that it is far from simple. You'll save yourself considerable heartache and headache by paying close attention as Lyndi walks you through each of these areas of your business.

No matter your goals for your business, I'm confident that you'll increase your likelihood of achieving them by embracing systems. In fact, just by being here, you've shown you're the type of person who invests in themselves and who values education; and that means you've already given yourself a sizable advantage.

Now go dig into the advice and wisdom throughout this book, put the lessons to work in your business, and multiply that advantage.

Keep going, keep serving, keep growing.
Clate Mask
Keap CEO and Co-Founder

IN DEMAND B.O.S.S.

Business Operating Success Systems
To Help You Get Organised & Save Time!

BY LYNDI MACRAE

First published in 2022 by Lyndi MacRae

© Lyndi MacRae
The moral rights of the author have been asserted.
This book is an Inspirational Book Writers book.

Author:
        MacRae, Lyndi
Title:
        In Demand B.O.S.S.
ISBN:
        9798365957756

All rights reserved. Except as permitted under the Australian Copyright Act 1968 (for example, a fair dealing for the purposes of study, research, criticism, or review), no part of this book may be reproduced, stored in a retrieval system, communicated, or transmitted in any form or by any means without prior written permission. All enquiries should be made to the author at *lyndi@lyndimacrae.com*

Editor-in-chief: Rachel Koontz
Cover Design: Sarah Rose Graphic Design

Disclaimer:
The material in this publication is of the nature of general professional advice, but it is not intended to provide specific guidance for particular circumstances, and it should not be relied on as the basis for any decision to take action or not take action on any particular matter which it covers. Readers should obtain individual advice from the author where appropriate, before making any such decision. To the maximum extent permitted by law, the author and publisher disclaim all responsibility and liability to any person, arising directly or indirectly from any person taking or not taking action based on the information in this publication.

DEDICATION

This book is dedicated to my three children Amie, Nathan and Ryan for being true to themselves and their dreams, for believing anything is possible and for shining their incredible light into my life. The difference you make to this world and to those you meet along the way moves me deeply. Thank you for being the most loving inspiration for me, I'm honoured to be your Mumma. I wouldn't be here if it wasn't for you!

And for you reading this book, #iBelieveInYou

TABLE OF CONTENTS

INTRODUCTION xvii

WARNING! xxi

SECTION 1 — IMPORTANT READ THIS FIRST 1
   CHAPTER 1: A Message from The Author 3
   CHAPTER 2: Business Automation Is Not a Dirty Word 9
   CHAPTER 3: Dreaming of a 4-Day Work Week? 15
   CHAPTER 4: Map to the Business Growth Journey 19
   CHAPTER 5: The Captain of The Ship 35
   CHAPTER 6: Is Your Ship Sinking? 43
   CHAPTER 7: Choose Your Own Adventure… 47

SECTION 2 — ALL ABOARD 49
   CHAPTER 8: Hello, Is It Me You're Looking For? 53
   CHAPTER 9: Here…Fishy, Fishy, Fishy 65
   CHAPTER 10: Get Your Net Ready 79

SECTION 3 — LET US ENTERTAIN YOU 89
   CHAPTER 11: It's A Date 93
   CHAPTER 12: Do I Have a Deal for You 111
   CHAPTER 13: Cash or Card? 121

SECTION 4 — DELIVER A HAPPY ENDING 133
   CHAPTER 14: Deliver on Your Promise 135
   CHAPTER 15: Gratitude for the Customer 143
   CHAPTER 16: Show Me the Stars 153

SECTION 5 — BUT WAIT… THERE'S MORE 159
   CHAPTER 17: The Keeper of the Lighthouse (Lyndi) 161
   CHAPTER 18: Freedom! 169

CHAPTER 19: Campaign Examples.................................. 177
WHAT'S THAT MEAN? CHAPTER TERMINOLOGY.. 183

"There's a big difference between
having a great idea
and implementing it."

~ Nathan Jones, 2022

INTRODUCTION

As every business owner knows…

Time is money!

This book will challenge you to be more efficient with your time by getting organised and show you a results-driven process that allows you to get more sales by doing less.

We all have the same 24 hours in a day, yet many of us don't use the time we have in an effective way to generate consistent cash flow. Instead, we tend to get in and do things we think are making us productive but what we are actually doing is wasting our valuable time and losing money.

The biggest problem I've seen and experienced in the online world today is so many people have a great front stage presentation to their business, yet their backstage is *shite*. It's disorganised, it's messy, it's inefficient, it slows things down and the biggest damage… it's costing you sales!

Take a deep breath in, and imagine…

How would it feel to know that what you have put in place is the backbone of your business and supports you 24/7 on autopilot? While you're sleeping, a prospect can access your information, connect with you and start to learn about you, your business and the results you deliver. And when they're ready, they can schedule a call with you, pay you money or join your membership portal. The main point here is they get a premium service follow-up each and every time and it all

happens, over and over and over… No B.S., no fluffery, and zero confusion.

It's an undeniable fact: you're in business to make a good impression and have a position of authority and recognition online. You want to be seen as the influencer—the go-to person for your industry.

Think of your business like a cruise ship. Just imagine if all the effort went into making the ship sparkle on the outside, designing the upper decks to be memorable and impressive but you have a clunky, annoying engine room trying to power the ship. You want the luxury ocean liner that delivers a delightful experience for all. Yes—it is possible!

There's a simple solution that will take you from disorganised and inefficient with clunky multi-system chaos to mastery using Business Operating Success Systems so you can take care of your customers past, present and future. Thus, you follow up with qualified leads consistently and efficiently which results in increased sales and repeat customers.

Which leads us to another painful problem for the business owner.

To return to our metaphor with the cruise ship…

As a business owner, you're the captain. It's your job to steer the ship in the direction you want it to go, making sure everything functions as it should.

However, just imagine if you as captain were trying to do it all: steer the ship, greet the guests, cook the food, mop the deck,

INTRODUCTION

make the beds, fix the engine, dress up to put on a show, *and* serve the food in the bistro and the fine dining.

All of a sudden, someone is yelling, "Iceberg!"

Better hold on… because it's all going down like the Titanic.

That's how so many business owners work in their business. They're too busy doing everything to keep the ship running that they don't notice when they're heading for disaster.

This is where this book and I come in. Think of me as the Keeper of the lighthouse, shining a light on the disaster you're heading towards. It's a matter of *when,* not *if.* If you feel you lack the systems needed to support your business growth, or you can't make a decision, use this book as the compass that shows you the way.

Does this sound like you?
Are you wasting time with repetitive, menial tasks?

Do you have to manually send follow up emails when someone joins your online program or registers for an event?

How much time do you take following up clients?

How many hoops do your clients have to jump through just to access information from you?

Are you going crazy stringing together a stack of systems that don't talk to each other?!

If you answered yes to any of these questions, you're about to discover a way to have the structure that systematically onboards, nurtures and entertains your future, current and previous clients—all on autopilot.

Keep reading and you will find out how!

WARNING!

Continuing to read this book will result in saving you at least one day a week in your business.

Only proceed if you wish to have more free time!

SECTION 1

IMPORTANT READ THIS FIRST

CHAPTER 1
A MESSAGE FROM THE AUTHOR

G'day, I'm Lyndi. In my world, online business is easy; it's my genius zone. It's my mission to shine the light on proven, results-driven processes.

I'm all about making it easier to do business with you online and delivering a happy ending for you and your customers. Clients come to me because they know that in order to scale their business to multi 6 and 7 figures they're going to need Business Operating Success Systems. They want their ship to run as smoothly as the voyage brochure looks.

For many years now, I've been the 'hidden gem' hiding behind the scenes for business owners, and let me tell you—all that time spent backstage has given me a wealth of experience. I'm always eager to shine the light on industry leaders and creative visionary entrepreneurs. Using a results-driven process, it doesn't take long to see the gaps, and this comes from real time experience, coaching and training hundreds of business owners from tech 'Eh, nooo' to "OMG! This is amazing… I have more time and freedom."

Together we've made their backstage (the ship's engine) rock just as much as the frontstage (the cruise ship). Having a beautiful website and online presence is just part of the equation in the *www* space. Sales come from marketing and systems make the sales happen more easily. This is where Business Operating Success Systems comes from, the complete approach—a holistic, end-to-end solution.

OK, I admit it. I am totally a tech nerd and absolutely love systems.

Over the years I've developed my own unique skills. I can see with X-ray vision into the backstage of your business. I can see what's going on; I can feel the fear stopping you from doing this 'technology stuff'. I know it drains your energy; I can feel it flowing out of you. I would feel the same way if someone came to me and asked to make their website pretty. It's just not my jam but give me a messy backstage that needs to be systemised and I am in heaven!

My job is to help you fall in love with Business Operating Success Systems or at the very minimum see the amazing value and need for them. (Let's face it, you can always outsource it to someone just like me who thinks it's so fun.)

I really love what I do, and I have fun doing it. I want you to have fun doing it too and get excited about the possibilities and what they will mean to you.

I HAVE TO LET YOU KNOW…

Be warned! You may be offended by the words in this book. It may call you out on what you're not doing, because I am a straight shooter and say it as it is.

You may go *blah* at the strategies and tactics shared here, perhaps you know better… I challenge you, however, to lean in and put your preconceived notions aside and approach this book from a place of curiosity and seeing what's actually there for you.

My invitation to you is to read this book with an open mind because you never know when an *AHA* moment will hit you!

IMPORTANT READ THIS FIRST

It's my belief that we can always learn something new even if we have heard it explained before. Just one sentence in this book could be the confirmation of the next step you need to take. That's happened to me plenty of times and I smile when I see the results one small comment can make!

If you're onboard with what's already been said and can embrace what is written on these pages with an open mind and heart, then you're ready to add automation into your business so you can scale.

Take a breath in and imagine…

Your automation system is in place and now supports you 24/7 on autopilot. Prospects can easily connect with you and purchase from you. They get high-quality customer service and follow up every time…No B.S., no fluffery, and zero confusion.

You've created a smooth engine and now your luxury liner not only looks good, but it's also a dream ship to enjoy the journey on. No more noisy clunky engine, no more patched together systems.

Now, a truth bomb…it's highly possible you may be like some of the creative entrepreneurs, consultants and practitioners I work with. You go *urghhhh* and shudder with the thought of having to do systems, marketing, sales, and administration!

I've heard:

- **Do I really have to be responsible to learn it?**
- **Do I really have to do this stuff?**

You may say what many have said before you, "I just want to focus on what I do". Or, you may think, "What I have works

well enough. I've put so much time and money into what I have, I can't change it now!"

What if the change meant an increase in ease and flow with how you go about business day to day? You could rest easy knowing each and every person receives communication and your message gets out there. What would that mean to you if you could rock out the marketing shiz!

What if it meant you could sleep better?

Would you be prepared to go through a little bit of pain to achieve so much more pleasure? Will you rip the band aid off what you have—a system that's not doing your brand justice?

Perhaps you have everything on one platform—your website, membership site, and some type of customer relationship tool that's been okay up until now. But you've always felt it's missing something. And that's the most important piece…the relationship building aspect, aka: follow up!

Smart client management not only makes you *look* good, but it also makes the recipient *feel* good! Have you ever been on the receiving end of a poor customer buying experience? I know I have, and it feels icky and you certainly don't buy from them again. You don't want to deliver that experience, do you?

Up until now, you've made the best decision from the knowledge you have. I'd like to pass on a bit more knowledge, so you are empowered to make an educated decision based on facts and not biased opinions.

Have you heard that phrase about opinions?

IMPORTANT READ THIS FIRST

We all have one!

When experience backs an opinion, it holds more weight. We can still make the choice; however it does need to be an educated choice and some will share a bright shiny sales pitch full of what you want to hear. Yet it falls down on what you really need. Their delivery sucks and you're left disappointed.

The web is full of opinions backed by money rather than what is truly beneficial for business. I don't blame you for feeling confused about all that's available.

This book is for you if you want to learn how using Business Operating Success Systems saves you time and supports you to create a smooth-running engine that carries you as far as you want to go. It will be the backbone of your business that allows you to share your story with the world, to reach the right people and deliver the right message using the right media at the right time.

Come join the elite and be in the top 5% of business owners who care about the relationships they have with their customers. You want to have a care factor and heart *and* still generate cash flow, because cashflow gives you the means to upgrade, scale and put more infrastructure in place and deliver more of what you love.

You're in the right place! Let's continue forward.

One more note, before we move on to the next chapter: there's a glossary at the back of the book where all the 'geek speak' terms used throughout this book are explained so you can understand the context of them and the use of them in this book. Please reference that section now, or anytime as needed as you read on.

CHAPTER 2
BUSINESS AUTOMATION IS NOT A DIRTY WORD

Automation in business can be great… when it's done right.

It creates a smooth slide customer journey experience that delights the end user.

Automation done poorly can create confusion in the end user.

A confused mind takes no action. Are you piling up the end user with overwhelm?

Automation can be personable and non spammy.

Many business owners fear losing personal connection with their clients. They know what it feels like to be on the receiving end of poorly done automation. When a prospect is interested, this is permission-based marketing and you back it up with attraction marketing— a strategy where businesses focus on showing customers how good the product is without telling them to buy.

When a prospect reaches out to you, they're interested in you or your services. When you're busy steering the ship, it's a challenge to check in on the passengers easily to ensure all have the same experience. That's why automated followup is important.

Let me share an example...

Sandy was connecting with clients, organising their consultation, requesting information, holding the consultation, then sending an invoice to get paid. Sometimes she needed to follow up for payment and offer ongoing support. She reached a point of exhaustion and thought, *this has to be easier*.

So, we used the same method taught in this book.

- Decide what you want the customer experience to be
- Determine what you want it to be like for the customer who's ready to engage with your services
- Write these down!

Once she wrote these down, it was easy to see...

"I want them to pay me, book a call, and send me the information I need so I can just show up on the call at the allocated time. I want to have packages I can easily sell for ongoing support."

And that's what was created. I call it a *smooth slide*. It's easy for Sandy now to send her prospect to visit a specific website page—they pay, they book, they provide the information. Suddenly, all of these steps became a lot easier and while at first technology appeared to be daunting and challenging to Sandy, it soon became the supporting assistant that took care of a lot

of administration in a personable way. The best part? This set up gave Sandy time and freedom to do more of what she loved.

WHY BUILD A LIST?

Have you ever heard this phrase? **"Don't put your eggs all in one basket"**, especially if you don't own the basket.

Imagine waking up to find your basket all empty: no eggs, no trace, nothing to recover!

It's something that many people don't think about when they begin their business. You know you need a social media presence along with other tools like websites and customer relationship management systems. However, what you fail to consider is…

Do YOU really own what you are building?

Those 10,000 followers on Instagram could be gone in less than a second if the owner of the platform decides your business violates their terms and conditions or, worse yet, if a hacker gets control of your account and all your hard work becomes their potential scam.

Imagine waking up and suddenly years of work and hours of effort—gone! Shut down overnight!

That sinking feeling is very real in that moment, as the blood drains to your feet, you go all lightheaded and dizzy, and you clutch at your chest as your lungs gasp for air as you've anxiously been holding your breath!

I know that feeling because it happened to me…

That loss taught me a big lesson, so now the ONLY way I do business for me and any clients, is that you're 100% responsible for all the assets, content, and systems. They are built inside your business ecosystem, and you're not held hostage. Your efforts to build your cruise ship are all yours, as it should be.

There are plenty of horror stories of business owners being taken for a ride, paying out big dollars and not getting what they paid for. It's these horror stories that have been pivotal in the creation of genuine success services we've delivered that allow you to shine and have time freedom.

What's peace of mind worth to you?

Own your ship! Be the captain, and have your deckhands support you.

What if you could follow a proven results-driven process to have peace of mind? You've got your ship, and by using this guide shining the light on what is proven to deliver results, connect you with your audience and make your life easier as a business owner. You'll have peace of mind and steering your luxury ocean liner, and your happy crew and the guests will love the experience you deliver.

For recognition and authority online, you'll need to create a solid footprint online and there's a way of doing that. This is laid out in this book for you too.

Peace of mind is having a duplicatable, repeatable, proven, results-driven process that will serve you time and time again.

IMPORTANT READ THIS FIRST

The Dream of a Business in Flow

Freedom is not the same for everyone, so what does it mean for you?

Does freedom from fearful thoughts of the clunky engine breaking down or sucking a lot of administration time sound like a dream?

If you have a clunky engine powering your ship, it's always going to be an irritant and not in flow. If you have a smooth-running engine, it's much easier for your team of trained, competent deck hands to take care of things for you. Initially it may be all you, so having a business 'automation assistant' is freeing. A team is much happier when they have an operation manual to guide them that you created. They can then do their job with ease and flow and receive praise and joy from you instead of a frustrated, grumpy sea captain.

Let's get into more detail about how to make that happen.

CHAPTER 3
DREAMING OF A 4-DAY WORK WEEK?

Being able to work 4 days or less per week—or to have the freedom to step away from your business for a holiday—is a dream for many, and it will only ever be a dream because of their own limiting beliefs and a lack of systems in place.

When you use smart client management and Business Operating Success Systems, you can actually do more while doing less! Getting organised and having small pieces of time saving automation you've created will make your heart sing, because you get time freedom to do more of what you love! Be it working less days, taking time off to go ashore knowing all the passengers on your ship will get the experience you designed for them already. It all just happens for you.

This is possible! I've witnessed many smiles and heard many squeals of joy, even sighs of relief as a load has been lifted. The vision and dream of the business owner becomes a reality.

It's also important to know, what you learn in the following sections are core principles and when done right, you won't have to rebuild everything should you choose to change direction. It's your engine.

> **Your ship is your business and it's yours, either a little rowboat that does the job or the luxury liner that gives a premium experience**

It's your choice where you decide to go. No matter the size of your luxury liner, using the customer journey mapped out for you in this book will support you. It's helped thousands of business owners scale their business and achieve time freedom. I'm revealing all you need to know.

If you don't want to take responsibility for your own business and be the captain of your ship and own your sh!t, close this book now, or better yet, pass this book onto a business just like yours, so they can get more leads, convert more sales and build a community of raving fans. Even if that community is small, you still can make more of an impact than you realise by using Business Operating Success Systems.

"You can make a difference one sale at a time!"

Now, you could stay doing what you've always done, or you can embrace the fact that a business needs sales and in the modern world, you can embrace technology to make it work for you.

You don't have to do it… only if you want to make money!

One thing that 2020-2021 has shown us is that in an instant everything we consider "normal" or "predictable" can be gone. All plans were cancelled, rebooked, cancelled again and again and again. The big takeaway from this is, we're all capable of adapting when we need to so why not jump in and steer the ship before a storm makes us adjust course.

What if?

What if you saw technology through a different lens? What if you opened the doors to new possibilities, would you dedicate

some time, embrace some discomfort knowing that this soon shall pass, and time freedom awaits you?

Are you ready to take charge?

Now is the time to take charge and be the captain of your ship, but don't be too proud to be involved because you don't like something. Be curious and be guided. Giving up the responsibility before making it clear what you want is a recipe for disaster!

Some captains send their deckhands in to do the work without clear understanding or direction and wonder why it flops. They're deckhands and want to do *what you direct them to*. They follow the captain's wishes, so the captain's input is needed. No one knows or *cares* about your business like you do and when you let others take over without your input, you'll experience frustration and you won't get what you want… which will likely confirm your belief that automation and tech sucks!

The truth is…

It's your 'I don't need to do this' attitude that is holding you back. This may offend; however, it's what I've experienced.

Results come from working with business owners willing to do the work, train their teams and have rock solid workflows in place that support their time freedom vision.

This book and the In2Web Marketing team are all about getting you what you do *want* and also what you *need*. It's a win, win, win situation, you and your crew (team) are happy, we're happy and the end users are happy. Yay to a triple happy ending!

Change may be scary, but it is not a bad thing!

Are you tired yet? Have you created a story to keep you safe? How long will you keep going because you're too stubborn and can't swallow some pride that perhaps there's a better, smarter way to do this thing called business and marketing automation!

Are you ready to shift gears?

Do you want to streamline your business systems, to start understanding and having some automation in your life that works for you?

Where you can start with taking what you already do, planning and documenting what you want and then automating some or all of it.

Now we are on the same page, let the journey begin as we create your map so you can navigate to create your customer lifecycle experience.

CHAPTER 4
MAP TO THE BUSINESS GROWTH JOURNEY

The 3 Phases and 9 Stages of Small Business Growth

Here's your results-driven process—guaranteed!

The 3 phases of small business growth provide you with a diagnostic tool that empowers you to find your gaps. Within each phase are 3 stages; each stage is a gap you need to fill.

Lifecycle Automation

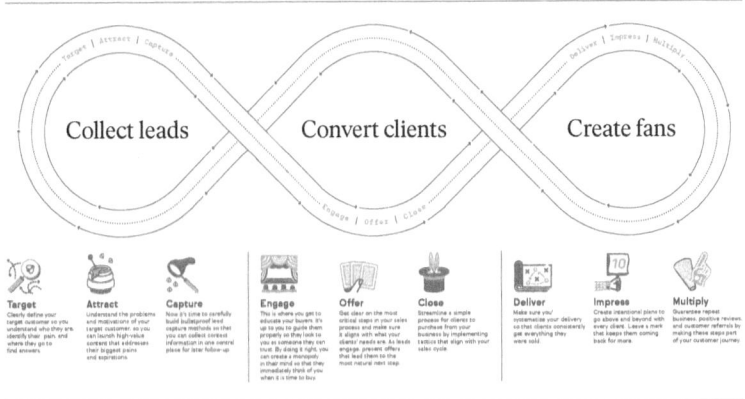

In each section of the book, you'll find a chapter summary chapter summary, use this like a checklist. You can also print off the Lifecycle Automation Self-Assessment located in the Resources chapter. When you print it and complete it, you'll know exactly what section to jump to in this book and what action you need to take next. The assessment is designed to help you focus. If you don't have access to printing it out, you could also use a note pad, post it notes and a pen!

This above diagram is your customer journey compass—the navigation tool that will enable you to be the captain of your ship. Use this alongside your map, a marketing action plan. With these in place, you'll have a smooth-running engine and your crew will love and be able to support you. Even if for now you're acting as the captain, crew, ship builder, fuel, the *everything*, remember it's possible to make a change! You *will* get there.

Let's go on an adventure

Have you ever jumped in your car and set off on a journey without knowing where you were going, how long it was going to take you to get there, where you were going to stay or how much it was going to cost?

Probably not. Yet each day business owners do just that with their customers. They do know what they want their customers to do, they want them to buy what they're selling but they've not planned out the voyage those customers will take to get there. Or if they have, there are gaps... it's a leaky bucket!

Here's the high-level understanding of the 9 phases to stages your customers will travel every single time they do business with you, even for repeat buyers.

When your customers set out on their journey, they have a need or a want. There is some sort of problem they have that's

causing them pain, stress, time, money, or sleep worrying about it. They know where they want to be but have no idea how to get there. This is where your business comes in.

When you travel, you need to collect data—so does the business who has what you want. The first step in any travel plans is to start making enquiries on a destination.

You go looking online, asking for input from others on where they went and what was good or not. Think about it. This is what your customers will be doing so you need to plan out their journey every step of the way even before they know they are on it.

It starts like this…

The destination is their **target** and they're thinking about what **attracts** them to that destination… so the online 'look up' begins. Eventually they filter through a lot of information and find their way onto a travel agent website and fill in a form— the business has now **captured** their details and their journey into the 'convert' stage begins.

The travel agent **engages** with them and provides some more information along with an **offer**. They may need to chat with them, meet with them, get some more information and they share some additional content that helps them make a buying decision and to use the service on offer. They accept the offer, and the **sale is closed**. But their journey doesn't end there.

So far, they've made an enquiry—some got a reply, and have been given attention and purchased the offer. The holiday is now booked. Some have made an enquiry and didn't get a reply and the holiday is stil la thought and the desire is left unfulfilled.

When a transaction is completed it's time to follow up on the purchase made. What happens when a prospect becomes a customer with you? What's next in their customer journey?

The person going on a cruise—they get to go on the holiday and now comes planning time.

If they're experienced travellers, they'll know what needs to be done, what luggage to pack, and what else they need to do to prepare for travel. They're confident, but a checklist and some supporting information is great to get too and makes it easier. It also keeps them engaged and excited about the money they just spent.

What if they're not experienced at travelling and it's new and this experience has them a bit confused and they want more information? There's plenty on the web if they do a search, but they'll need to filter out a lot of noise and irrelevant data to get to what they need and it can be time consuming and leave them exhausted, sometimes even frustrated. So why not setup an automated follow up process to offer some additional guidance? They'll thank you for it!

Think of the experienced travel agent that has created a pleasant customer experience, who has already sent some additional information to congratulate them on their holiday purchase and **deliver** an itinerary, along with other items that have proven helpful to a person who's booked and paid for a holiday. Now they ready to plan the experience to be the best it can be.

They're about to go on your holiday and the travel agent sent them an added bonus gift to use on their holiday too which was a nice surprise. They are quietly **impressed**.

When they return from the cruise, a follow up email asks for some feedback, which they're happy to give. When you get positive feedback, you ask for a **review**. The pleasant cruise experience leaves them happy to give a recommendation.

When you use the nine stages of the customer journey, you've plugged all the gaps to ensure every customer has the same delightful experience. This is how your business grows, with happy, content customers who become repeat buyers too.

Be the business that has a complete and fulfilling customer journey moving through all nine stages. It demonstrates you care about the end user experience.

But what if it wasn't that smooth an experience due to a lack of follow up? I could go on to share many bad experiences. However, I'm sure you can think of one or two not-so-pleasant buying experiences you've had. I sure can and it's these poor experiences that are fuel to my burning passion to ensure you understand the value of a happy ending!

It's your job as the business owner to prepare the journey for the customer long before they even start looking for the solution to their problem because when you do this, not only will their experience be exceptional, but they will also generate more sales for you.

How do you create your own delightful customer experience?

As the Chinese proverb goes, **"A journey of a thousand miles begins with a single step"**.

Let me ask you:

How easy is it for you to manage your business right now?

1. Can you turn on the advertising and have leads come to you? Can you follow them up without it taking any more of your time?
2. Can a prospect reach out to you and find a solution, so that they'll want to get to know you more? What do you have in place so they'll be hungry for what you offer?

If you find these questions relevant, then you're in the right place, right here, now reading this book. It all starts with first understanding what needs to be done—then doing it.

Business growth follows a defined path. We're all on our own journey, we're just at different stages.

If you're operating a business and have a $100k per month in revenue, imagine the revenue increase when you put this nine-stage customer journey experience method into action for you.

What about time freedom?

Start with automation of some administration. Make it easier for you and your team; this alone saves hours each week and presents you as an authority and industry leader.

What if you're at the stage of $5-10k a month?

My best advice, START NOW! This is the book I wish I had when I first started. Start mapping out what you do to deliver your service, this is the customer journey. I started using this method when I was at this stage in business growth and there

was no way I could scale and grow my business without the systems I use and it's all here for you. I focused on the deliver stage and used the smart client management system to stay in touch, deliver to impress and offer more and get referrals. There's no point in getting hundreds of new prospects and leads if you don't have a sales conversion process in place and can't deliver!

Knowing this process back when I first started like I do now would have saved me thousands of dollars and hundreds of hours of time that I can never get back. When you follow this proven methodology used by thousands of small businesses, you'll achieve more success than you thought possible - because of smart business automation follow up.

Create your marketing action plan (M.A.P.), get clear on what your next steps are. Then take inspired action and do it!

Let me just say, I'm not going to judge if your business backstage is a mess

Note: there is no right or wrong, it's all part of the adventure… I say this because, one occurrence I was working behind the scenes in what the business owner considered to be the BOSS (*Business Operating Success System*) zone, what I saw when I came on as the marketing manager was a BOM—that's Business Operation Mess! The staff were run ragged doing their best to meet the demands, yet they could never quite achieve what was asked of them. Or at least, not without stress and hustle!

They were offended when I suggested, "I'm here to take you from chaos to clarity." Upon reflection, what I should have said was, "I'm here to support your team and build Business

Operating Success Systems. As this is what I want for you, your team, and your paying customers."

Will the 'SHINY GURU' save me?

Good question…

The offended business owner poo poo'd the strategic marketing suggestions put forward and went ahead and hired a shiny object, smooth talking self-anointed GURU who charged a hefty monthly fee. The shiny guru borrowed the trophy title from another person—cheeky hey! And the offended business owner didn't see it. The business owner was confused about what they were actually paying for, what the team needed to do, how to do it and the shiny guru got them even more confused about what systems to do it in. I'm no shiny guru; however, I am a specialist in what I do these days.

If you already have systems, ideally you start with a diagnose and prescribe conversation, create a marketing action plan and work with what you have already.

We let the guru be the guru, I went ahead and created a system that generated $12k in just three weeks off the back of a webinar. These members were able to attend the webinar, click through to find out more about the offer, click and buy and were instantly in the membership area consuming the content. They also received email marketing that followed them up and kept them engaged.

$12k, fully automated and not requiring any team administration after it was set up! That's automating business like a boss! Using the systems they already had and the existing customer database.

IMPORTANT READ THIS FIRST

B.O.S.S. actually works! It's not a shiny object

What's a shiny object? It's like a pesty seagull squawking at you, persistent, in your face and written in a way that grabs your attention. Shiny objects can be a distraction away from what you really need. They sound easy, simple, and you want easy and simple… and building your own customer journey is simple when you know how. It silences the shiny objects, and you stop throwing chips at the seagulls and they stop pestering or distracting you because you have a plan, you have your map (compass) and have taken responsibility to be the captain of your ship.

It still blows my mind today at how blinded one can get when shiny objects are presented well, and I've had my fair share of shiny object syndrome. I've invested thousands of hard-earned dollars and been disappointed with what was delivered. These past experiences created a strong desire to create an affordable solution yet was still reasonable for the skills and knowledge required to develop such a system.

For me, money in the bank for my clients speaks louder than talking oneself up. Remember Sandy? She went from chasing up invoices to being paid upfront in advance. Ka-ching!

It's easy to get lost in the slick sales pitches that promise the world. I mean these gurus spend a *lot* of money learning how to SELL. They know how to trigger your pain points, to then promise you whatever they're offering to be the quick and easy solution to whatever is holding you back. More often than not, the great sales pitch is what the guru is good at and actually delivering what they promised falls far short. Now this is not to knock any particular "guru" or self-proclaimed "expert", it's just a major flaw in the current online business world.

It's my hope that you'll take time for you and put pen to paper. Draft your customer journey using the nine stages mentioned before and create your marketing action plan so you can see your gaps.

> *"If you fail to plan, you are planning to fail."*
> — Benjamin Franklin

CASESTUDY EXAMPLE: A business owner was faced with a problem and reached out as they had so many ideas and they didn't know how to fix the problem.

The solution was a mapping call and together we unpacked all the ideas into a structured format. By the end of the call, they had a plan, they knew what they needed to focus on first and said, "I feel so much better, I've got more clarity now and know exactly what I need to do."

If you find it hard to unpack your own brain and concepts into a marketing action plan. If you get stuck, reach out and we can create one together. During this process you'll learn about where your priority needs to be; it's then up to you to action it.

The Priority Pathway

The priority pathway is there to help you succeed and increase revenue! Knowing where to start first is not always obvious until it is. It may sound silly, however it's a recurring conversation and when it's pointed out. "Oh! So obvious," you'll say. Or, "what a great idea" is the response.

IMPORTANT READ THIS FIRST

Your priority is your existing customers and your existing customer database. They're often neglected because following up every customer who made a purchase from you is just too daunting!

- When a purchase is completed, do you stay in touch?
- Do you offer another service or do you let them know when you've created a new offer?

Your existing and past customers are the lowest cost leads to work with. Start there with an re-engagement campaign. This is a series of emails with content that delivers value, educates and informs them about your services, bringing you back into their thoughts. If they don't engage, you remove them and move on. You don't want to waste time on disengaged customers.

Many are afraid to contact past customers with annoying emails. They were interested and may be again, so are you saying no to potential sales because you're too scared to email them?

If a contact on your database no longer needs what you offer, they can unsubscribe from your database. And you want to encourage this—unsubscribes are nothing to be afraid of. **If you don't sell to them, someone else will**. It's been known for a re-engagement campaign to result in sales that were never thought possible. If you don't ask, you'll never know.

Did you know...

> **Depending on the size of your business, the total costs of replacing an employee varies from 30-150% of their salary.**

Many of the training calls I run, I'm amazed at how successful a business is, yet they don't have solid business operating success

system in place and this is limiting consistent cashflow. My mind races as we create their customised blueprint and M.A.P. and I get so excited for them. I know when they apply this proven methodology into what they already have in place, their results will be amplified.

My role is to ensure a smooth operation, so I know they will have the right engine to meet their needs that they can grow into and build on without too much disruption. I'm a realist and I know anything new can bring up all sorts of emotions.

You may have a successful business right now… yet you know it's missing pieces and you don't know what you don't know. Or you can feel your ship shudder and clunk its way forward instead of being a smooth-running engine.

You may feel you lack direction when it comes to marketing and business systems. Where to go next?

There are so many choices on offer and you don't want to waste your time or your money…

If you're like me, or the many motivated entrepreneurs that have walked this path before you. You've seen the gurus plugging their overnight success systems and how you can do it, too. You've most likely (like me) purchased many of these online courses, only to find they don't give you what you need, they are too generalised or they tell you to go buy five different systems to deliver the results. So, like many of those I've coached, you sit in overwhelm and confusion because you lack the guide that says… *do this next!*

Let me share an insider secret from a marketer's perspective.

IMPORTANT READ THIS FIRST

You'd be amazed at how many 7-figure gurus have all the polish and persona to speak to you from a video and sell you on their product, yet they suck big time on the delivery, the follow up, staying in touch, or just giving you what you were sold on. OUCH!

Sadly, it's more than you would know. They're proud of what they have (and rightfully so). It's just that they could be doing it better if they got out of their own way. Sometimes it's as simple as a seamless transition from acquiring a new lead and sending the appropriate follow up delivering the right message at the right time. The right system will make that happen on autopilot.

I've been behind the curtains of what appeared to be the top-of-the-line ocean liner ($1m + revenue) yet they lacked any simplicity or order and their team was overworked, stressed out and often felt deflated because it was really hard to deliver on what was requested of them. They had done their best with what they knew and had been told what to do by well-meaning gurus.

I feel for those crew members, and not only is it my role during the training to deliver what the captain wants, it's also to ensure the procedure manual is in place and the training manuals are current and supportive of the efficient delivery of the day to day business needs.

This book is based on a results-driven process developed by small business entrepreneurs for small business growth.

The beautiful thing about this book is, you take the generalised knowledge and make it personal to your business. It's almost like a plug and play system that is missing your content. It will have a framework that is versatile, a foundation so to speak, and you add in your touch to make it yours. You can use standard

frameworks to speed up the process, or you can do full custom builds.

You think it, then plan it, have the conversation with an experienced expert in the systems and go implement it. An idea has no value until it is tied to a delivery system to bring the idea from concept to cash.

From Idea Concept to Money In The Bank

When you can say what your idea is and what the outcome is, it's time to bring this idea to life. I call this the Concept2Cash method and it's part of the Business Operation Success Systems that'll give you back time and support you to streamline your business like a boss!

As a completer personality type, I work really well in what I've called the Concept2Cash method. One of my superpowers is hearing your idea of what you want and showing you the M.A.P. required that'll take you from where you're at, plugging the gaps and having full clarity and confidence of what step you need to take next.

To get to a 6- or 7-figure business, if you've been using systems to support your growth, it's time to do a check on the systems and ensure they're all running efficiently and serving you as expected.

Sometimes it means a review of one or a few of these systems, as you may have some crossover, some are now obsolete, or another may have improved and can now take over and help you to consolidate your systems from lots of different systems, logins and connections. To one system that can manage new lead collection, that will support you to educate and convert clients and build the community of raving fans.

IMPORTANT READ THIS FIRST

By now you've got an understanding of your customer journey and what it takes for them to find you, learn about you, build a relationship with you, choose to buy your product/service and love you so much they recommend your services.

Where do you find yourself?

On reflection, and depending on your marketing knowledge, you may find yourself across a few areas—either with the systems and lacking the revenue, or with the revenue but lacking the systems.

Fortunately for you, both of these situations can be rectified by you identifying the gaps.

Use the M.A.P. checklist in the resources chapter. Complete each of the 9 stages and put details of what you do now next to each stage you have completed. This then reveals the gaps or potential for improvement.

CHAPTER 5
THE CAPTAIN OF THE SHIP

It's time to put on the captain's hat.

Let's get you positioned as the captain of your ship.

Follow along this relatable journey to discover the treasure needed to improve your vessel.

What is your business like right now? Are you in a rowboat, a ship with a clunky engine or are you wanting to grow into the ocean liner? No matter where you are starting or where you want to go, it all starts with you putting on the captain's hat.

Time to take 100% responsibility for your actions and results!

This chapter is devoted to you taking 100% responsibility for your actions so you can get better results. When you take steps to market your business, it's a fine line of education, applying the knowledge and skill level to get the most out of the education and knowledge you have just gained.

Every captain needs a lighthouse

I'm the keeper of the lighthouse, and you're the captain of your ship.

What this means is, I'm in the lighthouse...let's dive into what a lighthouse does and what its purpose is. Stick with me here as it does relate.

So, on first glance, a lighthouse is a tall solid structure, wider at the base, narrowing at the top to where the big light is. This light spins around offering guidance to ships passing or coming into port, it's a guide. Sometimes the lighthouse is in the middle of the ocean where there are rocky outcrops, mostly we see a lighthouse on headlands.

A lighthouse can also symbolise the way forward

Let's relate the world wide web to the ocean, and you can surely feel lost on the web, just like you could be lost in the ocean. The ocean can get stormy— *really* stormy with white caps on the waves that threaten to capsize your ship. The waves will bash at your ship and test its strength and yours. There are times as an entrepreneur when you'll feel like you are drowning in the sea of the web, treading water and just coming up for a gulp of air before your head is under.

If you're not careful, and if you don't have a guiding light, this is where you can sink and drown, defeated and deflated, wishing there was a way that showed you where to go next. It's where you're just so worn out, you can't think yourself out of this one...however, the answer is simple.

Pause and take a breath in, and breath out with an audible sigh... do it again two more times. Breath in, hold, breath out. Breath in, hold, breath out.

IMPORTANT READ THIS FIRST

Now, it's natural to feel uncomfortable when you're in the water madly paddling to stay afloat, the water is lapping over your head and you're choking on it.

This same water will also support you to float... so pause for a moment, lay your head back, slow down your breathing. Visualise yourself floating in calm waters, the sun is shimmering across the tops of the water, glittering and so serene and beautiful. You relax, your breath settles and then you see the light flashing at you consistently, you know this light is just what you needed and it's saying... "Come this way".

Another beautiful part of the ocean is the squawking seagulls. You've heard them, right?

Squawk! Squawk! These noisy seagulls are what I liken to the shiny objects on the sea of the web. The distraction, creating a desire in your because it says "Get Rich Overnight For Free"… well, I might have exaggerated a tad; however, you know what I mean. The shiny object with a smooth-talking guru who is into hustle, grind, take your money and move on...to them, you don't matter so much and they leave a bad taste in your mouth. You might even associate all marketers to be just like them.

However, not all are created equal. While some of the content is similar, the teachings are there and there are multiple ways to achieve your results. Spreading yourself and your concentration thin will not support your best interests and get you to the happy ending you desire.

Now, let's go back to the ship, initially when you start out on your entrepreneurial business adventure, it's just you...and your ship is small, clunky and you've done the best you can with all you have. You could be highly successful and have a good turnover, yet there's a big block stopping you from upgrading

your ship, but at this point, you don't know what it is, you haven't been able to put your finger on it.

What's going to be the better way to go for me, and what does this mean?

This journey relates back to lifecycle marketing, lifecycle automation, Business Operating Success Systems and business growth strategies.

It's an undeniable fact, you know your business better than anyone else does, so it's your responsibility to have a handle on your business systems and how you deliver content to the end user and what that experience is like. You not only work in your business delivering the service, but you also need to do this marketing and sales thing, or at least have a system that allows your team (deckhands) to do what you want and need. If you give them free range with no system or process to follow, chaos ensues fast!

Be smart and develop smart Business Operating Success Systems now, just one little tweak like a smart customer management tool (the right one for you) can make all the difference and make your job so, so, so much easier. It's worked for me, and it works for thousands of small businesses. It's not an overnight success and it does require your effort in the setup/building phase.

You love your business and what you do, and you want to succeed, don't you? So, wouldn't you do whatever it takes?

If you're the "I'm too busy" CEO, then your team will be suffering in silence. I've seen it first hand with a big ego CEO

running what they thought was an ocean liner, and it may appear that way, yet inside the ship was a clunky engine and exhausted crew. Don't be that CEO!

If you're the "I leave it to my team" CEO then you're at the mercy of what they do. It might work for them, but what happens if they fall overboard? Do you have a life raft ready? Can you or any other team do what they did until a replacement is found?

If you're the "I can't make a decision, I'll let my team decide what is needed for my business" CEO, you're at the mercy of their knowledge, experience and expertise. Do your team members have enough experience to really know your needs, or are they doing what is comfortable for them and not necessarily what's best for your business growth.

Is it possible a conversation with one who specialises in systems would be the better choice?

A mentor of mine has said it many times, so much so, it became ingrained in me and now I use it to determine who is qualified to give me advice:

> You go to the person that has five times more experience than you in that particular field. You want the person who stands at the top of the mountain or close to it, so you can get the best advice. It scares me when I hear the comment of relying on what the team recommends… what is their real-time experience? Do they really know how to scale and grow your business? How many years of experience do they have, or will they keep themselves safe and recommend what they're comfortable with?

To run an ocean liner (those really big fancy ones we escape to for a fabulous break away from busyness), imagine all the crew,

all the systems, all the different moving parts required for it to run ship shape. There's a lot, right? Each person knows their role well; there's procedure manuals, ongoing training, there's even drills for the passengers in the event of an emergency.

Running your business (both offline and online) is the same—there are a lot of moving parts you need to have in place. The good news is you can start with low-cost, affordable systems that will grow with you, or you can use one system. If you then find it's not quite doing all you needed, change is required. Sometimes a complete engine rebuild is needed so you can deliver a pleasurable experience for your end users. You don't want to drown them in your chaos!

If you have an ocean liner that has the appearance of what you want, yet it has a clunky engine, isn't it time you took inspired action and made a decision to do things better so you can have a smooth-running ship? Then you can have all your team able to do their role easily and efficiently. Keep reading as this book will reveal potential gaps, and you may go, *Erk, ouch! Yeah, she's right!*

Just perhaps maybe you need to rip the band aid off and switch engines and build a smooth-running ship that meets your needs now and will grow with you. Just because you've invested time, money and effort into building a clunky ship, doesn't mean you keep persisting with a clunky ship, it's time for a better engine. Your passengers deserve that much from you.

It's time to do the work laid out in this book and see the rewards of the guaranteed results!

Note: If you hand over the control to an under qualified crew member, or if you don't have documented business operating

procedures for your crew to follow, your ship is going to run aground or go off course. Before you know it, a world of pain gets you and you have an even bigger job on your hands.

Take heed of the warning, just barging your way through the reef will cause unseen damage. Rushing to make everything pretty without the right systems will lead you to a clunky engine that your crew get by with, but is it as efficient and effective as you want it? Don't let your ego get in the way. Have that conversation with one who has five times more experience at that 'thing you need' fixing. It makes all the difference.

Do the work, take the right actions, this is how you can 'scale and then outsource' what you do. If you outsource work to your crew before you have a procedure manual in place, before you have good operating systems in place. It may still work for you. Like the *'I know best CEO'* said, "I wouldn't have $100k a month turnover if I was in chaos."

Think about what's it like for the crew, the passengers? Are they having the best experience, so they become brand ambassadors or raving fans? Leaving it for later can be a longer and more painful process to unpack everything into some order to see where you're at in your business development and it will cost more for sure! Mess in the technology space is always harder and more work to pull apart and repack, so do it now; make a start.

Use this book to connect the dots of what you have now, see what you could do to improve still and more importantly what you really need.

A good captain has earned the position, is open to feedback and changing course if required. Like a good captain with his map, he plots a course, and sails off with his crew on a mission…

he has clarity and purpose and has a fine sturdy ship with an engine that hums.

What kind of ship are you on?

Let's take a moment and visualise yourself standing at the helm of your dream ship (your business). It feels good and you feel the power beneath your feet as the boat powers easily through the strong ocean currents of vast ocean. The crew go about their tasks and your ship runs on autopilot mostly and the manual steps are never missed. You have full trust that all is in order. It works like a dream with ease and grace and can easily upgrade when you need to without great pain or changes required.

Ahoy me hearties, away we go!

CHAPTER 6
IS YOUR SHIP SINKING?

Let's assess your ship using **The Online Footprint.**

If I was interested in your business, and I Googled your name, what shows up?

Creating your online footprint leaves a stamp on the web; it's you claiming your place to share your message.

Does it build confidence in me that you're congruent with what you do?

There are many ways you can leave a footprint and there are many tools you can use too.

Your online footprint includes your personal brand and your business brand; they both matter as an entrepreneurial business owner in service. Your audience wants to know who you are and what you stand for.

The front stage of your business is where you have what attracts WHO you want to serve. This includes your brands message, website, social channels, and others' websites you're featured on.

The backstage is hidden away from public eyes to see. They need to opt in to get access and you have control over this. The backstage is where your automated follow up sits.

The hidden follow up system is where you can share exclusive content that's not open to all. However, creating a digital footprint and doing it the right way from the onset (or adding to what you have in place now) will save you time and money. It'll gift you back time to do more while doing less.

Have you dreamt of working less? Well, business automation will support this to become a reality, to manifest it using the strategies in this book.

Use your website as an online brochure and entry point into getting to know you. It can appear to be simple yet have the power of a customer relationship management tool as the engine. Your website is one place you draw a line in the sand and place your flag. *Find me here!* it says.

And to take your website from an online brochure to a lead generation marketing tool for you. You connect every form into your smart customer relationship management tool (CRM). This I call automated marketing websites. They become the salesperson that never sleeps and work for you, without you needing to do anything.

An established business with a high turnover that lacks systems may also lack a digital footprint, so imagine if you do a few tweaks a little at a time.

Keep in mind that you can't plant a tree and expect fruit the same season, you plant the seed, you water it, you nurture it, and it grows and eventually fruits. You don't expect instant results. Marketing is a bit the same, while there are some strategies that can get you fast results, you want to have three to five core high value offers that you've taken the time to refine and have proven to be attractive to your audience.

IMPORTANT READ THIS FIRST

How long could you sustain responding to all who visited your website and then sent you messages and emails? What is the experience for them waiting for you to respond going to be like? A bit rough, right! And it's totally avoidable and now you have zero excuses. Can you do all of that ongoing manually when you're servicing clients?

You need the gift of time freedom! Put aside the "Errgh, *tech*" thoughts and say to yourself… "*I really want my time back*", if that's you. Then, now is your time! Don't wait years and have hours of frustration because you are confused. Get a mentor to support you and work with them, commit and dedicate this time for you now to achieve your time freedom (the fruit from your tree).

CHAPTER 7
CHOOSE YOUR OWN ADVENTURE...

Not everyone reading this book will be starting out at the same place and that is perfectly OK. No matter where you are in your business development, you can choose the perfect place to start. The following sections and chapters will allow you to choose your own pathway to success and go to the section and chapters in this book most relevant to you now.

Hopefully you read the "Start Here" chapter; this is written to give an overview of the entire book and get you thinking about what you're currently doing or more importantly not doing. If you haven't already, read Section 1, Chapter 1.

Do you want more leads?

Head over to Section 2, where I've outlined the three stages for collecting leads.

Do you want to convert more sales?

Go to Section 3, where I share the three stages for converting clients. This is where you can engage your existing customers and this is the starting point of your priority pathway.

How do you create raving fans?

Learn how in Section 4. Discover how you can deliver, impress and multiply. The delivery stage is a key follow up piece and automation can free up your time here significantly. This is my favourite stage to develop using automation as it's powerful, personalised and super-efficient. This is where you deliver a happy ending.

I know you want to make a difference

Me too! I'm grateful you're reading this book… because a business needs a solid foundation to succeed and be able to grow with grace and ease. To be able to scale, your business needs Business Operating Success Systems in place. You'll do this if only you're seeking time freedom. You'll do this only if you want marketing strategies that support you in understanding your customer journey and creating a pleasurable experience for them.

You want to be free to focus on new connections, sales and delivery of service rather than chained to the wheel of administration and lead chasing to make a sale.

This book is about the business foundation building blocks. It's about the journey your end user (the prospect or the customer) goes on. And you get to be the captain. *If you build what's included on the pages in this book, your business will succeed.*

For me, there's nothing more inspiring than a creative entrepreneur with a big heart on a mission. The drive and passion to create a transformative result grabs my attention. It's an exciting moment when clarity hits.

SECTION 2

ALL ABOARD

The goal of this section is to help you feel confident in knowing who your ideal customer is and where to find them. You have leads consistently taking action to learn more about your business, and you have a frictionless method to systematically add every contact into a single system to immediately follow up.

Collecting Leads

If you answer yes to any of the following statements, you need to read this chapter!

1. I need to attract more customers to my business
2. I don't know exactly who my best customer is, so I'm trying to reach everyone
3. My potential customers don't have a compelling reason to buy from me

All Aboard!

By now, your ship is ready for boarding, your business is ready to start finding people to experience what you have to offer. Hours have been spent on product research, money has been spent on websites and staff and you know what you have to offer is just what people need.

"Build it and they will come" was great for the field of dreams but unfortunately in real life where there are hundreds of thousands of businesses fighting for people's attention. Just getting ready is not enough.

Neither is simply shouting, "All aboard!" at the top of your lungs. Just imagine if that was how a cruise ship planned on filling the vessel.

Does the captain shout from the top deck to what he hopes is a full pier of eager, cashed up, ideal passengers who are ready to just throw money at him to take a trip?

How likely is that to happen?

So many business owners get trapped in that same notion that if they have a product that is great, then it will sell itself. It won't.

Strategic planning and effort come into play here, not only to create awareness for what you have to offer, but to attract the *right* customers.

The ultimate goal is that you confidently know who your ideal customer is, and where to find them. You can then communicate with your prospects with ease and flow giving you time freedom.

Collection of leads is the first basic step you need and of course it can be done manually; it can be done in a messenger chat. Or it could be done in a customer relationship management system you've customised to you, your brand and your business needs.

Remembering to Use the Right Bait!

When you go fishing, you need different bait for different types of fish.

You can catch a fish with a standard bait, or you can use one that you know they're hungry for. Which one will be easier?

If you're just starting out, there's some work to be done setting up lead collection. Set it up right from the beginning and it'll pay off for years to come.

If you have been in business for a while now, you may have developed your own way of collecting leads which can be tweaked, or you've been fortunate to have run a referral-based business up until now.

> You may have created attractive lead magnets to test the theory of what will attract your ideal client's attention, only to find out you're using the wrong bait and heading in the wrong direction. It happens often that there's a gap between "thinking you know" and actually knowing what they want. Or you may need to test and measure what converts to find what really resonates with your audience. Remember the fish and bait!

> Are you ready for qualified leads consistently taking action to learn more about your business, and do you have a frictionless method to systematically add every contact into a single system to immediately follow up? Many don't and that's okay too, now's the time for smart client management.

> New leads, hot prospects, or existing contacts require your attention, repeat engagement with your existing contacts with attraction marketing methods.

No matter where you are starting, right now is the time to review and start to build your complete customer journey.

CHAPTER 8
HELLO, IS IT ME YOU'RE LOOKING FOR?

Let's talk about how to target your audience and attract their attention, then send them the right message at the right time!

There are two important times to look at your audience:

1. When you're doing lead generation to get new leads
2. When you're segmenting your existing list

Knowing who you're targeting with your business is important

Kinda sounds obvious right?! Now, as you're here, reading this book, you've most likely been delivering your services for a while, or at least, you'll know what your ideal customer looks like, what their fears, wants, needs and desires are, and you'll know how to speak to them. Remember, communication with your prospects and customers is full of insights. They will tell you what their needs/wants/fears/desires are without even knowing they are doing it. This is *marketing gold!*

Lead Generation: The Prospect

The prospect is someone new to your business and quite often new to the solution on offer.

Think of it like the first time someone books a cruise. They know they want to go on a trip, in a boat, on the ocean but they have no idea what that is going to involve. They have an idea and a desire to do this. It is your job to show them that not only do you have what they want but also that you are the *only* one to give it to them.

A new prospect needs education, they want to learn about what you do, why you do it and if your offer will solve their problem.

This is where a lead magnet can filter the new prospect through to a series of emails that educates them. In marketing, this is known as an indoctrination series of emails. It's where you share more about services, results or case studies and you share about your business and how it can help them.

You then move them through to a long-term nurture campaign that you deliver value to support them. These are a weekly email and I'll share a content creation strategy in the resources later in the book.

Ding! You've Got Mail!

Why send emails?

Simple, to make sure your time and energy goes to the people who really want what you have to offer and by the time you step in to give them your attention, they'll already feel like they know you, like you and trust you.

Lead generation with your existing list

Already have a list? Well done!

Existing customers who've worked with you, and purchased your products are the treasure in your business. Place a big X marks the spot, then your M.A.P. will lead you to them again and again with new offers (you'll have 3-5 main strategic plays - remember this is a results-driven process). Existing customers are the ones you want to nurture and keep informed with what you're up to.

> "You don't earn loyalty in a day.
> You earn loyalty day-by-day."
> - Jeffrey Gitomer

Like all good relationships, you have to put in the time and effort to keep them strong. Having the expectation that if they like you, they'll follow you on social media is a bit presumptive and an expectation you have that leaves the customer who loves you neglected. What if they miss the opportunity to work with you again because they didn't see the post you made?

It's actually easier to sell to your existing customers than to new ones

Customers who have worked with you already know you. They like you and they trust you. They know what they're getting with you. Human nature is attracted to reliability and consistency; change can be scary. There are fast food chain franchises worldwide and when travelling you can go there and know, a burger will be a burger. It was designed that way to give you peace of mind. You know what you're going to get. We can learn and use what is proven to work and adapt it to add our personal touch. It's the concept that's important to observe here.

To keep in touch, you must have a way to update them and sell to them with nurture emails. A good mix of content, promotion and entertainment in the sequence will not only keep them on your list but more importantly have them look forward to you showing up in their inbox *and* opening the emails.

If you have content you're posting to social media, then this content is what you send via email to them first. Treat them as a VIP. Let them know first and this VIP list becomes a list of hot buyers for your programs, and they move on to become brand ambassadors which we talk about in the multiply section in this book.

Neglecting the fundamentals will hurt you over time

The fundamentals of marketing are required and when you establish a healthy habit that becomes your unconscious competence, then you'll achieve that which you desire. Creating processes around what happens for the new incoming leads to take them on a journey is proven to increase your bottom line. Start thinking 'attraction marketing'! This is where the prospects are magnetically drawn to you, they devour all the content available to them because you've made it easy.

Just having a website full of blog articles doesn't mean prospects will consume them, that's too much effort. You assume they know where to find it and how to find it and what to search for. (And as I'm sure you've heard, "when you *assume* you make an *ass* of you and *me*".)

You must make it easy for your prospects

Easier for you and easier for your prospects and you can repurpose the content you have very easily and efficiently too.

The web is full of content, we have content overload these days, everything I write about here is somewhere online for you to go find... but that's time consuming and you don't know what to trust as there's lots of 'shiny objects' blinging for your attention and they can put you in analysis paralysis! Thus, you take no action and here you are today, years later knowing you need this... yet you've not taken the action required because... What's the real story going on for you here? What's stopping you?

If you try to be everything to everyone, you end up being nothing to no one. It spreads you thin, it leads to burn out! It's not the path you want to go down; it's perceived to be easier, so it's more attractive, however, if you can speak directly to your audience and get to know them well. It's easier for you in all areas of your business.

Generalist or Specialist

There's a growing trend in entrepreneurship to niche your business to a specific audience, this will attract your 'target' customer when they're looking. In business marketing, for example, a business owner will choose to work with a business that works within their industry; it's just easier when the style of your business is understood. Niching also leans towards a specialist. Have you ever heard the saying 'success leaves clues'?

If I offered you everything web related you could do (that's a massive list by the way), like I used to, just to earn income... you wouldn't know how I could help you or how you could refer me to one you know needed what Lyndi offered! So, by being the master of your craft, knowing who you want to attract. Being specific in your messaging and speaking to who

you want to work with… It makes your life easier and also your prospects too.

There's niching in a few ways, and you can get very narrow, when you get narrow, this means you can speak directly to that person's pains and needs. You validate them and they feel safe, and this is where building of the relationship starts. If you don't give them a smooth prospect experience, what's your customer experience going to be like? You can set the standard you want from the onset.

A confused mind takes no action

Please don't confuse your prospects; instead, give them a clear path to follow. Doing this also makes it easier for you to collect leads because you know *who* you want to attract. While it may feel weird, you have to take them by the hand and guide them exactly where you want them to go, what actions to take and even remind them to pay you.

Take coaching, for example

There are many coaches coaching in different niches, for specific ailments, there's coaches for the coaches.

When looking for a coach, you'll find one that has industry specific knowledge because they know the industry and can speak to it on a deeper level. It's even better if the coach is a specialist in your industry. For example, I choose a mentor who has at least 5 times more experience than me in that particular thing and their values align.

> **"Pay once, cry once" ~ Mal Emery**

Find a mentor or coach that's compassionate to your needs while giving you enough stick to get shit done! This is much better than fluffy feel-good words that don't stretch you. What you're creating has to be uncomfortable to a certain extent, and I don't mean physical pain, I mean you're stepping out of your comfort zone and into the unknown space of technology, it can be a beast. That's why having someone in your corner can be a game changer, to tame the beast. It's new to some, and new is change, new to the ego mind can bring up fear… again, a good coach will support you to move through this.

If I was to reflect back on the courses I bought, the mentors I've had and where the best results came from. It was definitely when I invested heavily in a specific thing to achieve an outcome. I've spent thousands of dollars on courses that I've never opened as I bought into the front cover presentation and the backend didn't deliver. I paid my money and never heard from them again, until they wanted me to buy from them again. Those people got my money, for that one time and that's where the relationship ended. Why? Because they didn't have a customer journey in place, they just wanted money, I was just a number - or that's how it felt to me. One of our basic human needs is to feel valued and respected, even when making a purchase.

Do you give value once you've got clear on who you want to target, I'll talk more about that in the next two chapters.

An example of a niche business that does it well

Back in 2020 a friend told me about this online book writing intensive and said I should come along, and I did; however, I

wasn't ready then, though I did write 30,000 words in a week and some of that is blended into this book.

What attracted me first off was the name 'Inspirational Book Writers' whose title speaks to the right audience immediately. The content shared (the marketing message) is specific and clear and this content is attractive to those ready for what is on offer. Inspirational Book Writers know their target audience.

> "It's a sniper specific target rather than a shotgun approach"
> ~ Lyndi MacRae

When I joined the Book Writing Intensive again May 2022, I was all in! I went to Dave Thompson from Inspirational Book Writers because of the process he'd created and the support that was there. Writing a book is one piece, publishing and launching is the next piece and it also has many moving parts. I chose to go to the man at the top of the mountain. Investing in the right support is needed and you can't expect things to happen overnight. Adding automation to the backstage requires a strategic approach and planning, so that's why starting now is better than putting it off for later. Business automation doesn't happen overnight! However, you can see results in as little as 5-8 weeks! This I can 100% guarantee you.

One last thing on the book writing intensive. It was a deeply transformational experience that has evolved how I do business, and I highly recommend it!

It helped me gain insight as I observed my own actions as a business owner with a project I wanted to complete.

In my travels on the web, looking into book writing, I also saw some book publishing training for under 100 bucks that promised to support me to write a book. My thinking at the time was, *more information is a good thing, it will help me!* I bought from them, paid and kept going with my busyness and as I write this, I've never accessed the materials because I can't find them. I have no idea who I got them from, I have searched intensely and I'm tech savvy! It was deflating and not inspiring.

These offers attracted me because I was looking for that thing right then. The big promises filled me with hope and guess what, they never delivered. They actually left me uninspired, anxious over not being able to find any communication from them about my purchase or how to access it. You'd think 'publish a book' would be in a follow up purchase email somewhere! Nope… so, when I put that failure aside and put my focus on Dave, guess what he and his team did—they delivered on their promise and they sent follow up emails.

Writing a book requires a series of steps, it's not only the writing of the words and knowing how to create an easy-to-read book. There's a lot of knowledge learnt over time in the tech setup, the process, the cover, the edits… and as a backstage systems mentor, I know what's involved. It's why I knew I didn't want to know all the backend stuff on publishing a book, I wanted to work with an expert who could take away the pains and frustrations and do it for me. I don't need to do it all myself, but I *did* need to take responsibility and take inspired action.

A niche business will serve you *if* you have a backstage that matches a front stage. And if you manage with what you have, imagine if you could add in a few new options to deliver a delightful experience for those you attract into your business.

You want to deliver a happy ending!

Yes! That's right, you want your prospects to feel happy...

Business Operating Success Systems are about setting up business development foundations that will grow with you or make what you do in the day-to-day business operations easier. You take what you're doing now and evolve it. We do this all the time, so it's easy and we support you one step at a time to understand how this results-driven process will support you—the customer journey is real! You must know what your customer lifecycle is and create the journey, knowing you'll need to test, measure, tweak, refine. Remember the smooth slide.

When you have an idea you want to bring into reality, and you'll have the basics mapped out, even if they're in your head. Through conversations, we unpack your business brain into a proven formula. It's one of my strengths that I love doing.

A building without solid foundations will crumble

A beautiful luxury ocean liner's engine will fail if the wrong parts are used.

Imagine trying to power a luxury ocean liner with a 5-horsepower engine. It will get you started however it can't sustain the momentum needed and in time, it's going to give way. The same thing happens with your business if you don't include a solid backstage (the engine).

Will your business be sustainable and make the 3-5 year 'successful business' milestone?

Setting yourself up for success with smart client management will support you to run an efficient business. Your beautiful ocean liner will not only look good, but it will also run well.

Even if you've been established for years—many are missing what I speak of here—so you're not alone and it's not a failure, you've been busy serving your prospects and customers the best way you can. Developing your own Business Operating Success Systems is a way to expand beyond what you do now, while remaining personal, it can help filter contacts as well, so you get rid of tyre kickers and freebie seekers and positions you as the authority in your niche. It also sets your prospects up for success when working with you.

Having Business Operating Success Systems will give you time freedom and ensures a delightful prospect and customer journey. You'll be fully aligned to do more while doing less.

The goal is to ensure you meet all 9 stages of the customer lifecycle your contacts move through from prospect to customer and onto brand ambassadors who tell others about how amazing you are!

Think about your existing customers, why did they connect with you, is there a theme across your ideal clients.

Who do you really want to attract? What do they care about and where do they hang out? You're going to need to be clear on this so you can post your Lead Capture link to be in front of them.

CHAPTER 9
HERE...FISHY, FISHY, FISHY

Now we know *who* you're wanting to attract into your business offer. What's your bait?

What's juicy enough to capture the attention of your ideal customers?

What gets them salivating with their credit card in hand?

Is it easy for them to pay you?

Does completing a transaction require your input, or can the end user do it automatically via your website or from a link click in an email you've sent? With the right systems in place, they simply click and engage with your offerings.

Creating a way to connect and engage with you

There are many 'things' you can offer. The ultimate answer comes from delivering your service and getting results. This will reveal to you what works and what doesn't. Whatever it is you have, that thing must solve a problem, you need to position yourself as the solution for their pressing need. You do have to give it a go and put in time, effort and energy into the creation of what you believe is most attractive.

However, from an end user point of view, you need to put yourself in their shoes. They're lying in bed, scrolling on their

phone, or going about their day. Remember this often as you sit to create your content… who are you writing to, where are they hanging out, do they like a certain style of connection?

If you think that offering them something "free" will be enough to get them onto your list and start the relationship, think again. Your prospects know that nothing is really *free*. They may not be paying you money for what you are offering but they are giving you something. Their email address and permission to sell to them. If they *really* want what you have to offer, be it the freebie to consult or freebie to purchase, they'll give you their genuine email address, if not, you'll get the junk one where all the unwanted marketing goes to die. You want a way to repel the tyre kickers, the time wasters who will never buy from you. This is where low-cost offers can help.

> **"Ignoring online marketing is like opening a business but not telling anyone."**
> - KB Marketing Agency

Somewhere in all you do every day are golden nuggets that are very desirable to your end user. Go create, test and measure. Once you do this and gather real data, find out what engages them the most; then, amplify that thing.

So how can you use educational direct response marketing to attract more prospective customers?

Let's use the following list of agreements you'll make to yourself for your business growth for effective and efficient marketing— it always comes back to following proven strategies and tactics.

Here's a list of 10 attractive attributes of great marketing

1. Always: Use a highly targeted list
2. Always: Create a compelling message with clear, benefit-driven sales copy
3. Always: Make an irresistible offer
4. Always: Give clear, specific instructions on how to respond
5. Always: Have fast, multitouch, multi-media follow up
6. Always: Have tracking and measurement
7. Understand marketing and business math
8. Build a sexy ship (marketing systems, not just one-off campaigns)
9. Commit to, acknowledge and respect the connection you have with your clients and target market on a regular and consistent basis
10. Commit to making your service or product extremely valuable, not just improving your marketing

Many of your prospects have fallen prey to substandard services, even with freebies… they opt in and never even open up the message that is sent to them. What was the point of them getting it? In that moment it caught their attention and if you can engage with them at this time, if you can get them to open the email and consume the offer, you're more likely going to close the sale.

Getting prospects to opt in

Visualise your beautiful attraction piece the prospect is going to be captured by. This is the top of your funnel, and we'll move down through the stages.

Your freebie offer should be an educational piece that delivers a transformational outcome. It solves their needs immediately after they engage.

The cold prospect finds you because you're using attraction marketing and targeted efforts to get your business in front of their eyeballs.

You can only rely on referrals and organic traffic for so long before you need to step out into the big wide world and say, 'Hello, come look at this' and naturally a bigger ads spend budget will make this easy.

The opt in and never open

If prospects are doing this, it generally means something needs to change on the thank you page (in the next chapter I'll dive into why this page is one of the most under used pages in a funnel).

Ways to attract the prospect's attention…

What can you do to bring these prospects into the top of the funnel?

You can run **Google ads** (a business presence on Google must not be neglected here either) or do cold calling aka telemarketing (it still works when done in the right way but it's still a 'use if you must' option in my books). Cold calling is not meeting a person where they're at—if they're not looking for your solution, it will be rejected. So, for the unaware prospects who need what you offer, this is where your attraction marketing efforts will pay off. They'll naturally be drawn to you.

Referrals are always good and are considered warm leads to join your funnel. Joint ventures are a way to connect with those who have your audience before you do. Where are your prospects before they need you? Can you do anything for those who work with a big pool of your ideal prospects?

How often do you see posts asking for recommendations for a service? Trust through association warms up your prospects and makes the conversation easier. So having a way they can jump into your funnel and start to digest your content happens without taking up any of your time, yet you know it's delivering the exact experience you want. It lands a prospect in your lap educated about you and your offerings. Having someone else you trust recommend a product or service to you, cuts through your defences and has you clicking "add to cart".

Direct mail is the old and familiar snail mail; we don't get much of this and lumpy mail is a great way to stand out in the good ol' letterbox and create some delight and childlike excitement as it's like receiving a gift—when in reality, it's just really good marketing done right!

Your **website** is a lead generator for you; it provides information and as discussed further down, all forms on your website need to link directly into your smart client management system and send follow up automatically.

Networking events can be great for making connections, do you have a way to collect leads, add them to your smart client management system and follow up?

It's really easy to set up a small piece of automation here to add the lead into your smart client management system and send a 'nice to meet you' email that invites them to engage with you

further and get to know you more. There's a lot of opportunity here!

> "The best marketing doesn't feel like marketing."
> -Tom Fishburne, Founder & CEO, Marketoonist

Press releases always drive a lot of traffic when done right. For these, it's good to work with a PR expert to ensure a quality written piece that delivers a clear message with a strong call to action that you've setup specifically for these leads. Why? So you can track the source and see what your conversions are like!

Trade shows get you in front of a lot of eyeballs and these prospects will get bombarded with follow up. It's important you have some compelling copy written and in place and a way that these leads can instantly connect into your emarketing system to get connected right away. (A simple competition campaign is great here as you can get them to validate their email to confirm their entry.)

Seminars and webinars are in-person events and online events. With these, you're speaking to a captive audience of people who want to know more and have already put their hands up. Having an event follow up campaign is beneficial and simple enough to do when you work with a smart CRM.

Newsletter marketing can be a powerful tool. You can email multiple times a day, weekly, monthly, or at whatever cadence you choose; however, email needs to be consistent and deliver value. With the campaigns we set up, we always include a way the end user can stop those emails but not fully opt out of all marketing. Legally, all mass sending e-marketing systems must include the unsubscribe link at the bottom of every email.

The **cold prospect** doesn't know you, doesn't yet trust you and doesn't even really care about you or your product yet. You can change this more easily than you would believe.

Providing a Quality Resource

You want to ensure any information you give your prospects—such as a free resource, audio series, or video—is instantly delivered to them. These prospects then become what are called a warm leads and using direct response marketing brings them into the top of your funnel. They're clearly interested and may or may not be ready to buy now. Only 3% are buy now ready. 70% need to gather more information to make an educated buying decision and you do that next.

Other elements your attraction freebie should deliver

- Establish you as the industry expert and authority on the subject
- Stir up dissatisfaction about the current situation (problem) they have
- Educate the prospect about their options and how to buy, what to look for
- Answer FAQs and overcome objections
- Provide case studies, testimonials or other proof elements to validate your claims. You saying how good you are isn't enough!
- Sell the next step in the sales process, either a free call or completing a purchase. Both are transactions that require follow up

You could jump on the latest shiny object that's trending and see how that works for you. It may burn a hole in your pocket.

Or perhaps you could develop your own 3-5 core strategies you've tested and proven to work for you. See some strategic campaign examples in chapter 19 for some ideas and create your own success pathway using lifecycle automation. Remember it's a results-driven process!

We'll continue on with the 'funnel' in the next couple of chapters, so keep reading to find your answers.

Up next is the how: how do we collect the leads and build a database of qualified prospects... we're moving into my favourite place to play and where using the right tools will support you to easily and effortlessly create all you need for a smooth slide end-to-end solution.

A lead generation strategy example

Let's take this book as an example. It's what Dave calls my 'front door' and is created as a guide and resource to share what we do at in2Web Marketing. It's designed to work with existing clients. It's also created to get the attention of new prospects to educate them and if they want to know more, they have the knowledge on how to do that.

Your attraction piece is part of your strategy, that leads your prospect towards your training or service, plus any tools (modalities) you use to deliver the result which delivers the successful outcome.

STRATEGY + TRAINING + TOOL = SUCCESS

Shout out to Greg Jenkins of Monkeypod Marketing for that little string of words! I've found great success with this formula, and I know you will too.

For years, I've always said I like to work with motivated entrepreneurs. Entrepreneurs have grit, they show up and do whatever it takes, even if it's kind of like visiting the dentist and it feels like a teeth extraction process! Entrepreneurs move through it, and they never give up.

> **"Never give in. Never give in. Never, never, never, never…"**
> - Winston Churchill

So, how do you get your prospect's attention?

Simple. Your message must deliver a result or benefit your prospect wants, or it stirs up uncomfortable feelings they may be feeling by not having the solution you provide. You'll need to create content for your website, for your emails, and for the social channels. You can use the content creation strategy I share in the resources to easily create yourself nine blogs and this exercise takes you about ten minutes max to do. From there, you write a blog, take a snippet of that to your nurture emails and from there you post onto the social channels. And it can be done ahead of time and scheduled so you don't rush.

Using the customer lifecycle workbook available in the resources chapter, you have a marketing action plan and idea on what your focus needs to be. You can combine the content creation strategy and lifecycle automation with a M.A.P. (marketing action plan) so you have clarity on what you're working on next.

You always need to have a **call to action** (or CTA) where you can 'capture' the lead's name and email then offer your follow

up message. There's an old saying I've heard floating around for years… **'The money is in the follow up'** and it's true. I'll plant a seed here for you to be familiar with the concept in the next section where I dive deeper into 'nurture emails'.

Here is a useful copywriting tactic from a training session I attended with Steve Plumber in 2014.

PROBLEM | AGGRAVATE | SOLVE | PROOF | ACTION

In 2015 I would write two emails a week for a client. 104 emails per year is a lot of work but luckily I was able to tap into the PASPA method.

How?

From building a list of over 400 questions direct from the audience. Those answers became the content of future emails, so it was no surprise they converted from email subscribers into seminar attendees and then became members in a $25k mentoring package.

The emails spoke to the problems they were having and the offer was the solution.

When they saw the JOIN US IN PERSON button, they clicked through to a webform and selected the venue and date to attend a live 1-day event. They then entered another event follow up sequence that contained 'stick emails'.

Just because they clicked to say, 'Yes, I'm coming' doesn't mean they will. Your job is not done here; more on nurture content in the next section.

Let's pause for a breath

Phew! It's sounding like a lot of work here already, and if it's new to you, it can leave you sitting in a feeling that's unfamiliar and uncomfortable.

Especially if you're a creative type and technology, sales and marketing strategies and tactics are not your jam, when tech and the know how eludes you or at the time, you understand, but then when left to your own devices, you get lost and don't go back and complete the next step.

This is where you'll benefit most with a guide, be it in a group situation, having access to training videos in a member area for you or your team to do it yourself or be the VIP one to one call time person who likes a personal experience with done for you frameworks you can add your message to, or hand over everything to an experienced team.

Where you go depends on your goals, your skills and what you're prepared to do. It's fun to have a chat and get clear on this and it will unlock so much for you and give you clarity.

After a Marketing Action Planning and strategy call the feedback was this: "Thank you! I feel direction again."

Prior to the call, we'd been implementing some systems to put out the immediate fires and solve current pains that needed swift action. There was some confusion around how all this marketing automation, business automation and new system setup could work. Once the fires were manageable and the urgent goals put in place, we were able to pull back to PLAN the next most needed item and with a M.A.P. this business owner knew what was coming. They also knew they had a

guide to keep them focussed and not running down the wrong rabbit hole.

How would it feel to have a strategy that works for you? A map.

Work on the strategy in this book and develop the Lifecycle Automation & Marketing pathway for your prospects and customers. Then implement them into your business.

"Pay Once, Cry Once"

One of my early mentors Mal Emery used to say, "Pay once, cry once" because of his years of experience, knowledge and know-how and he charged $25-40K for his premium service. You paid for his years of experience, knowledge and know-how, it was then delegated to a team, done for you and you just had to approve. You have the map here to guide you to do it yourself. There are plenty of ways you can build your own sales and marketing engine!

As I bring your awareness to the 3 phases of business growth and the 9 stages your customers will travel, with follow up in place, they become believers in you. And as you take inspired action and get the right system so you can follow up, nurture and educate and maintain an engaged audience, I'll see that as a success. If I can inspire you to make one small change that improves your day, I'm happy. Leave a review on how this book has supported you. One time step is all it takes to create a ripple effect transformation and get you back on track.

I see a lot of paralysed business owners who are committed and dedicated but have a lack of knowledge and understanding that is standing in their way. This is why these "do it with you" programs are great; not only does the end user learn and

increase their knowledge. Like learning anything new, you need to invest some time (or delegate it to an educated team member to do it for you) to get it right from the start.

I've seen many reach the point of extreme frustration and want to cancel everything, simply from not staying focused on why they wanted to improve their systems in the first place.

Tapping into the industry experts and paying them for their experience to fast track your learning can be worth it. Get the supported call time to walk through and complete the setup with confidence, until you've built up some knowledge and courage to have a go yourself. Hence, pay once, cry once.

Now, let's just briefly circle back to your lead magnet, and what you offer.

Can you answer the question, who is your customer?

Do you ever think 'everyone needs what I offer'? While that may be true, the situation is likely more nuanced. Your audience wakes up thinking, *I need 'a specific thing'* – they know what they want. If they go looking for that thing, will they find you?

If you're thinking *'Everyone needs what I offer'* is that really true?

> "Build something 100 people love, not something
> 1 million people kind of like."
> - Brian Chesky, Co-Founder & CEO, Airbnb

While I know all businesses need Business Operating Success Systems. Not every business is my target market. It's a rapidly

growing industry and gurus pop up overnight from having studied a course and done some of the setup and they bought into the 'you can do this and sell this and make money'—in other words, it's affiliate marketing. Sell a concept, get them to buy the tool and they'll have instant success!

Erk, puke! Sadly, this scenario is more common than we think, and while these gurus do get paid well, they also have a high refund request rate and leave a trail of unhappy burnt-out businesses along the way.

- To wrap this up, ideal prospects will come knocking at your door when you attract them by speaking to their problem with a message that resonates with them

You'll need a way to collect the leads, convert them to clients and create a community.

Read on for what your business must do!

CHAPTER 10
GET YOUR NET READY

A leaky bucket won't hold water, and a net with holes in it catches no fish!

When a prospect is attracted to your offer, you need a way to capture their details. When they complete the form, landing page or schedule a call, they become a hot prospect, so every touch point matters.

When I first started learning about direct response marketing, there were 7 touch points… now with the changes in how we interact, and because there's so much more noise, it's between 12-22 touch points. We need to have additional pieces of information, content emails that deliver value and all of them should include a strong call to action (CTA).

This means you need to carefully plan out your interactions moving forward and be patient because while you may get the unicorn customer who just whips out their wallet and buys everything you have the very first time they meet you. Chances are, it'll take time. I mean, you wouldn't ask someone to marry you on your first date especially if it was a blind date. Red flags would be flying all over the place.

You want your freebie download, seminar, or sales letter to position you correctly and have them eager to work with you.

Here we are, we have our Lead Magnet created

We know *who* you're attracting, we know *what* we're using as the bait… now it's time to fish and get the bait onto a really appealing and sexy hook. What will your irresistible bait and hook be? It must be congruent, it's not the bait and switch tactic that's been used in the past!

You know, I know…we all know these days, when you enter your email into a form, you're going to get emails because of taking that action. This is known as permission-based marketing and it's one of the most reliable and consistent methods for highest conversions.

How to catch a fish as you collect leads

To capture a lead, you need a form; that form can link to a static result or it can link into your automation tool of choice.

A static form means when you fill in the form, it shows a brief thank you message and sends you an email. You need to be at the inbox when that email comes in, so you don't miss it.

Is your inbox crazy like mine? I get over 150 emails a day, mainly because I opt in on purpose to see how different companies have their automations structured. Russell Brunson made the term 'funnel hacking' popular and more known. I called it and knew of it for years before and have been doing this for years. It's called reverse engineering.

Reverse engineering means you can look at existing systems and messages and use that knowledge to recreate a similar system. You create your marketing with the end goal in mind,

and work backwards from what you want your new prospect to do.

Another example of a common 'static form' and one that's used for lead generation is the well-known, and often misused, website 'contact us' form.

Automation Opportunity!

The website 'contact us' form can be the most used form on your website, so why not leverage it and add a smart form behind it that helps segment your list, gather data, and ensure you're reminded to follow up with them. This is a hot lead!

This is nearly *always* (much to my dismay) set up as a static form that sends one email and the lead just falls through the cracks, unless you have an attentive sales team member who's delegated the responsibility to follow up on these leads. Even then, without an easy way to track the leads, the sales team can miss hot leads too.

Many small businesses may not yet be in the position to employ a full-time staff member to monitor the sales channel. And some have them working from a spreadsheet. Unless you're good at spreadsheets, it's hard to keep track of who needs a call, who had a call, who was called and a message left and a reminder to call them again the next day. This is where a sales pipeline steps in and supports you (more on this in the next section).

Until you have the spending budget for a dedicated sales team, you can manage by using a smart CRM that not only affords you some smart client management, it also affords you lead capture, sales and marketing follow up and more using planned strategic tactics after you've completed your marketing action plan.

Ready to game plan your automation?

If you want to claim a M.A.P. session and get a game plan to revolutionise your business, visit: https://indemandboss.com

Your website can be turned into a salesperson that never sleeps, simply by hooking it up with your smart CRM. This is known as integration and there are many 'techy' ways to do this. The simplest is taking the form and adding it to your website; however, most businesses want the forms to style to match and blend in with their website. And this can mean getting assistance with a web developer or tapping into a team that can do this for you.

Adding a webform onto your website contact us page is better to be a 'direct into CRM'.

> *If you don't know the term* CRM, *please refer to the glossary at the back of the book where all the 'geek speak terms' are defined.*

What every business owner wants and what every business owner needs What we want to have happen

Have a prospect visit your website and head to the contact us page, this prospect is considered already an engaged and interested prospect. It may be existing clients or customers who use this form, if that's the case, your CRM if smart enough will not trigger anything fancy a second time as you setup the pathway and included a way to filter out 'current clients' who've already been through your 'get to know you' (GTKY) sequence.

Converting a prospect into a lead via your website contact us form

The prospect goes to the website, fills in the form, contact is added to smart CRM, smart CRM uses automation to complete the processes, you preconfigure the follow up emails to run based on what you want to happen. You get a task notification; the lead now sits in your pipeline and a task awaits completion.

In the ideal world, every web developer would offer this setup when building a website, however they don't. I speak from experience and understanding, as I'm speaking from a web developer background and building what I termed 'automated marketing websites' Otherwise your website is an online brochure that's not working for you. You want your website to be a lead funnel into a smart CRM.

An 'automated marketing website' simply means, every form on your website leads into your smart CRM and triggers the team to follow up. If you don't have a team, it sends you a notification to follow up.

With setting up business automations, you invest time and dollars now, for greater returns month on month for years to come.

Do you feel that's worth it?

What sort of business do you want to build?

Put time in now, start with the basics and then grow from there when you have a deeper understanding of any specific nuances. Then sit back and reap the rewards time and time again as you smile knowing the process you set up is working for you, to support you have the best and most active list of contacts.

Now, back to the lead capture… the white paper offer

A freebie download, video, request a quote—whatever your thing is—needs to have a sequence of pages connected that takes the lead from one place to the next and it all makes sense for them, the message is clear and congruent. They feel comfortable and are happy to hand over their personal information to hear from you—because they are filling in the form.

To capture your leads, you need a way to collect their name and email at minimum, and phone number is better so you can call them (the website 'contact us' form can easily get away with the phone number being requested and required, simply because of the placement of that form).

A landing page is a place you have content and a form for the one thing on offer. This page is known as a direct response landing page. There's only one action the end user can take with you— well, two actually: one is to complete the form and the other is if they click away, you may have tracking pixels on them for retargeting ads.

On your landing page, you want some key elements to entice the viewer to take the action required on the page they're on.

Does your headline call out loud enough, does the rest of the page content all support and provide a compelling reason why they should give your details.

> NEED HELP?
> *At the time of writing this book, Keap has an amazing tool released for Keap users, it's called the Keap Copy Generator and with this, and the amazing 'how to play blueprints' you really can do a big chunk of the framework and content creation yourself, in very little time!*

Wooah! All that 'techy talk' is a lot to take in, in a short amount of time only because it's new to you, trust the process that you will get the hang of it, it will not feel like you are reading a foreign language. Give yourself time to embrace the learning.

Let's pause for a moment and take a breath in… hold for 4 seconds, breath out for 4 seconds… repeat this 3x's. I've just thrown a lot at you, and depending on your understanding of marketing, it can all be a lot. I can still get overwhelmed with the complex automations and these may be needed later on, start simple. Simple automations will save you time. Simple automations with real life applications in real businesses with real customers…*this is the space I've played in since 1996*. How can you use automation to solve problems and leverage the technology we have, and this thing called the world wide web.

Right, now you've caught your breath, let's keep moving along.

- You've now got your landing page visualised
- You have your freebie giveaway item
- You have copy for your landing page and now we need to think about what comes next

It's perfectly understandable if you jumped to—send email and deliver the freebie thing with a link! You're not alone in thinking that, and you're partly correct; however, there's one more *really important* step before that, and it's one of the *most neglected* components when setting up a marketing funnel (even the website 'contact us' form needs this piece).

Do I have your attention…

Any guesses on what I'm referring to above?

You'd be correct if you thought of the **THANK YOU PAGE**.

I can't stress enough how important this page is. Think about it and feel this…

> *The lead has just filled in a form to get what you offered. The next page is the thank you page. It's on this page you have a hot opportunity to communicate a clear message to get inbox engagement, to ensure the lead knows where to go next, what to look for and what to expect. This page is perfect for a video to walk them through what comes next, to offer an appointment, or to redirect to another page.*

It would be like someone asking you to fill out your information to enter a raffle and once you did, they just stared at you. No "thank you", no "good luck", no "I will add this to the barrel and winnings will be drawn on this date". Just someone frozen in time staring into space. You kind of wait a second and walk away feeling confused and a little distrusting of the whole situation.

USE CASE EXAMPLE: Sandy wanted a better way to manage her client bookings. They reached out to her, and she booked them into a call, had the call and then had to follow them up with an invoice, then check the invoice was paid and chase up payments more often than not… because humans get busy hey! We don't intentionally forget; there's only so much we can do in a day.

SOLUTION: We used her smart CRM, from her website the end user clicks a link to PAY for a service, then is redirected to BOOK in the call. So, she now gets paid before the call proceeds and she's delighted and it's so much easier for her to do business for herself, Sandy now spends less time chasing an interested lead. Sandy took the time to build a lead generation/conversion system and it's working well.

Another tool that makes it easy to direct a prospect to a form!

A positive business outcome of the 2020-2021 pandemic, was people had to learn to use **QR codes** so much that now they are normal in everyday life. QR codes failed when they first came out in 1994, I remember attempting to use them in the early 2000's. Most people didn't know how to use them, so I stopped until now! Even LinkedIn has a QR code to jump directly to connect, so why not have one on a flyer a person can easily go from offline prospect to online lead directly into your smart CRM.

The same goes for Zoom. Everyone you speak to now has heard of a Zoom meeting; it was how we could all connect and meet from our homes. This style of meeting was not new, back in 1996 I ran a chatroom using a platform called ICQ and there was also MIRC and a few others. These days it's a lot easier to meet online and there's many tools available, you will find what works best for you.

Another way of collecting a lead is through appointment bookings

Using an online scheduling tool really does make it easy for the prospect to find a time that suits them to talk with you. No going back and forth in emails or messages trying to find the right time. A busy business owners time limited, so by offering an easy and efficient way is actually respectful rather than impersonal. And of course, you want follow up email to follow up when the appointment is made, any extra communication or requirements gathering. There's some smart follow up you can create here and what that is depends on your needs.

In this section we've talked about your target and who, we talked about attraction and how to capture the lead… you can access additional resources on the website: https://indemandboss.com

Some additional food for thought about collecting leads…

- *What will attract your potential customers to engage with you?*
- *How attractive is your ship and cruise experience?*
- *How easy is it for your customers to do business with you?*
- *What will you do to get the right prospects' attention and generate enough interest, so they develop the desire to get more information and take action right now?*

SECTION 3
LET US ENTERTAIN YOU

The uncomfortable truth: If you're business, you're in the business of sales.

You are also in the business of building relationships so you can establish authority and trust, leading your prospects to become clients.

Attraction marketing leads to easier sales

We don't like being sold to; we do like to buy... get this right and sales will happen naturally.

The goal of this section is to help you consistently convert leads by following up in a timely manner while educating prospects about your services. You want to have a strategic and intentional sales process that utilises effective offers to close deals. You also want a way to regularly engage with those who might not be ready to do business today so that your business can stay top of mind.

Converting Clients

If you answer yes to any of the following statements, you need to read this chapter!

1. I don't have great content or strategy to get customers to buy
2. I don't know how potential customers make decisions on what to buy
3. I need to improve my sales processes

Let's be edutaining to make more sales

That's education and entertaining.

What's the convert stage in your customer journey now?

When you take what you're already doing and unpack the process, this creates your business standard operating processes.

What do you do once you have captured the lead? What comes next? Most businesses stop here and are leaving money on the table. Or some switch over to "I don't have time so I'm going to spam you with offers in hope you'll buy"

This is where you'll be guided not to jump to a *buy my thing* piece of communication either, as much as you want to close the sale right now. The prospect needs to be ready. We'll touch on 'ready or not' and how soon is too soon and how you can use automation to make this feel nice. Yes, you heard me right, how you can make it feel nice for your prospects to want to give you their hard-earned cash!

When you make an offer, how do you do it?

- **Have you thought about creating hot sub lists** so you can send them the sales letter style emails and continue to educate the ones not quite ready yet!

    Now that's super sexy and appealing as an end user don't you think… feel that power, when you can send a personalised email that's on point for where your potential customer is at.

- **You want the porridge temp to be just right** to get the happy, content customer sitting back smiling that they invested in you. And they'll thank you too

- **How do you go about closing a sale?** Can I go to your website and click to buy, can you easily send a quote, invoice or take payment over the phone and set up a subscription payment or do I have to email you, chase you up if I want to give you money?

Do you say NO to more money?

There are so many horror stories I could share on this one!

There are many different ways you can go here. Read on to see what you do now and what you want your end user experience to like...

How far off are you from that?

CHAPTER 11
IT'S A DATE

"Approach each prospect with the idea of helping them to solve a problem or achieve a goal, not of selling a product or service."
- Brian Tracy

Where all good leads go to die!

I have to be honest with you: this chapter is where most business owners fail.

However, as you're here, you don't have to join the statistics and if you've been guilty of doing this in the past, you now have the way. This is the way to connect and engage and educate your new leads…

HINT: YES! This leads to more sales

"Building relationships converts more sales."
- Lyndi MacRae

The music is playing, you're feeling good…

When you have automated follow up in place, it gives you greater peace of mind that no matter what time of day… whatever it is for your end user, they can get your best version of you. They can find out about you and consume the offer they signed up for, because you've taken the time to create the best possible connection, giving value and helping them see you as the beacon they desire and have them hot and heavy to shove their credit card at you.

Mmmmmm, feel that delight for all involved.

Insert the sound of the record that was playing a beautiful tune to suddenly scratch to an abrupt end! *Eerrwupfff!* You're jolted out of the delightful feeling…

Let's expand on that jolt feeling as that's how a lot of businesses with amazing front stage presentations go.

How does it normally go…

The Horror Story: They didn't want my money!

Here's an icky connection experience I've had, and I know you've had.

Imagine you're sitting in the seminar watching the presentation. You already knew this person so there was no relationship building needed, you trusted them and were sitting there with credit card in hand, ready to drop some cash their way.

You approached them after the presentation all enthused about the buying decision you had just made in your head. They look at you quickly and say 'hi' and then thrust at you a paper form

and are told, fill this in, give it back to us and we'll follow you up next week… and they move onto the next person.

How do you feel? Me personally having this experience with someone I knew, I felt deflated as I wanted to get what was on offer. I wanted to leave that day knowing I had invested in me, and this offer was my next focus to grow my business.

A few days past, I had not heard anything, so I dropped a messenger message to them and the reply… "I'm flat out and I'll get back to you."

Okay, so I sat waiting for the email that never came. The relationship was now broken, the trust dwindling because I believe in being true to your word. Have you ever not been able to follow up a prospect because you're so busy with paying clients that you can't deal with new potential clients?

Did they not want me as a customer? Or were they just too busy?

Did they ever get my cash?

No! I did spend my cash elsewhere though as I'm always growing the business and sharpening the skills sword, as we all should.

Okay, so what if I didn't know them and I didn't have the trust. I would have been a lost lead, a prospect that was hot and ready to hand over cash. I mean, if you're presenting at an event, you're doing it for lead generation and sales. So, you want to make sure you can connect and follow up anyone who approaches you and not leave anyone out in the cold feeling disappointed.

How many get this experience from you? Do you even know?

So how can you do this differently? Simple, you start with a warmup sequence of emails that flows on from a 'nice to meet you' networking event follow up sequence. The paper form can be an online form, I could have filled it in right there during the presentation. Then my details could be sitting in the follow up funnel, added to the sales pipeline, a task created to follow up me up and I would not be forgotten. And all of that could have been done using automation.

Wouldn't you want that for anyone ready to invest in your services you've just presented?

Let's look at the relationship building and how you can educate and engage with prospects

Let the nurturing begin….

It goes like this…

Congratulations! You've got an email of a hot new lead and it's time to start building that relationship. The best way here is to imagine you're meeting someone for the first time on a date. Think about how you would go about this meeting.

Think back to your dating years, what was better, getting to know the person, gaining trust and developing the relationship before you went all in.

Or was it all about them, they wanted to skip the trust building and relationship and just get what they wanted which left you feeling dirty and *euwwww* no thanks.

A business transaction is very similar.

Let's flip it so you're the customer here, as I want you to feel their experience so you create a pleasurable experience for your prospects and customers.

Let's imagine you're attracted to this person, and you're going on your first date. You show up, you have a conversation, you share information about you (they share about them), what you like (what they like), what you do (what they do). You laugh, smile and the relationship building has started and you're in the early days for trust, as you're still feeling a little unsure. If all went well, you part ways and with any luck, you get a second date.

The second date comes around and you hang out, chat, and share more. You build on the relationship more by sharing information. During the sharing of information, you're building trust... Can you see where I'm going here?

If they jump in on the second date and are invited back to their room, before you've had a chance to build up enough trust (or desire) then it's possible you'll give them a slap and end the date there!

It's easy to push too hard too fast and this can lead to your date (prospect) feeling offended, simply because you jumped at them too fast.

How do we avoid the 'slap'?

We avoid the prospect slap by creating a smooth transition from what they've requested through to building on the relationship.

Now, you could be thinking, I do this on social media, I do messenger chat and I... whatever it is for you. What I'm asking

you to do, is to take what you do now and improve on it. What can you do better! Can you write a series of emails that positions you, your services and creates curiosity in the reader who is left wanting more. How long this takes varies from business to business and also depends on if your prospect is qualified for your services at all.

This is where the prospect can 'get to know your business services' through a series of emails to build a deeper relationship which will lead to trust. You may not have the time to have conversations to satisfy their curiosity about you. So why not let them get to know you through a delightful 'get to know me' series of emails - there's a time and a place for talking about yourself and there's a time you make it all about them! You want your prospect to be warmed up and open to your offer. If you make an offer too soon, you can get the opt out, reported as spam or give the recipient an icky feeling as they weren't ready.

As you know by now, I like talking about Business Operating Success Systems and for me that includes a quality customer relationship management (CRM) tool. Creating a smooth experience for the end user is a non-negotiable, it's paramount in avoiding the pushy salesy buy my thing way that creates an undesirable experience!

Relationship marketing and having the prospect come to you hot and heavy for what you offer. They see their pain going away if they choose you, because you've already given them some value and demonstrated your expertise and authority to be the solution. You're now desirable.

That's a good feeling, however it doesn't end there.

You have my attention, now follow me up!

I don't know about you, but I love it when I can go looking for a thing I want, and I can request more information and put in my email to get it sent to me. I can consume some right there if they have a killer **thank you page**, I know I'm in for a smooth slide. If the thankyou page is non-existent, I know I'll be lucky to get any follow up from them.

They've only partly got it right. If I get follow up, then I can work out 'if' I want to book a call, buy the thing—I can find out more about them and if what they do aligns with me. Some businesses have excellent marketing in place, and I'm sent emails, some a bit too many, some I don't hear from.

Who do you think gets my money?

Using a smart CRM, once you've captured your prospects' attention, they've filled in a form and have received and consumed what they requested. You can progress them along in your funnel to the 'action takers sequence' (meaning they clicked to download) when they have taken this action, you can speak to them differently to what you would one who has not yet taken this action.

What happens most of the time, *and it's not wrong*. Most of the time, it's set up to deliver the download and that's it.

Why is this?

1. It's the marketing tool in use that doesn't offer automated follow up
2. The business owner doesn't know any better and they're scared to send emails because they don't want to be pushy

If I walked into a physical shop, and the shopkeeper just ignored me and didn't offer any help in finding what I needed, I would just walk out. When a shopkeeper pays attention to me, asks what I'm looking for and makes some suggestions or directs me towards what I'm looking for I'm delighted as I feel valued, it makes me happy to spend my money in that shop. If I'm there to spend money, I will welcome the guidance, if I'm just browsing, I will say, "Just looking."

Online connection is just as important as a shop front

I put my hand up saying I'm interested, and you left me hanging!

I might be ready to buy right then, but you've now lost the sale. I might be looking into what I want, but you've lost the sale because you didn't offer me anything of value.

What if you attracted the ideal prospect, you captured them in your net, and that's where you stop! Do I just die in the net all alone?

Ummm, hello? Is there anybody out there… just nod if you can hear me, is there anyone at home?

What if there's no more connection or communication between you? You're in the business of sales, remember!

You need to build a relationship so those who want to buy now can, and those who're just looking can continue to browse without effort.

What if you had written a few short emails that meet a person where they're at, even with a download, you acknowledge that they have downloaded the resource and you can speak more directly. Here your follow up emails go deeper into relevant parts of the resource you've delivered, that they have opened and consumed. For example, you remind them about what's on page 2 and the benefit it has if they do it.

I'm sorry, there are no excuses with all the tools available to you today!

Using the e-marketing tools available today, there's a way to connect and engage in a personal way that leaves the end user feeling acknowledged and their time respected. Plus, they really did want to get to know you some more to work out if they want to do business with you. And because you made it so easy, you win their trust, and they will gravitate to you. The beautiful thing here is that you also will repel those not suited to you and what you offer. It works when done right!

Hello, attraction marketing…

Whatever it is for you, write down what you want to have happen…this is your first and most important step in business automation and it's actually a requirement if you wish to scale your business and have the team support the day-to-day business operations.

Start where you're at, what you're already doing!

If you haven't unpacked what's in your head into a clearly defined process, how do you expect your team to know what

you want and support you without it being painful for them. In the resources section you'll find a link to go complete this unpacking exercise. It's not always easy to do yourself and sometimes being asked the questions to then be told, go write about *xyz* is easier.

It's more common than you'd believe that a business owner has not documented their process clearly. Surprise, surprise... Is this you? And it's okay if it is. Another recurring pattern I see when clients show up for our training calls is, they don't know where to start. They may know they know it, yet they've never documented it and have no clue how to automate it.

And again, I'll say, 'That's okay' it's where we guide you, and teach you the skills you will use over and over again and develop the muscle memory so it's no longer a painful experience. We chunk it down, unpack it and then get you thinking… if they do this, the next bit is… if I do that, the next bit is… This is the 'if this, then that and dance' you'll become very familiar with.

If you don't know what your customer journey is, specifically the Convert Clients stage. How can your sales team, or how can you as a busy business owner manage it all yourself if it's not easily visible and manageable.

What do you do about that?

You simply start where you're at now and write down the steps for each stage of your sales process, in detail and then you have the beginnings of your operations manual which you may need at some point when a new team member takes over that position.

It's often a belief that you think you don't know what your process is, however that's not reality when the right questions

are asked. As this is an individual thing for you and your business it would be wrong to say. This is where *xyz* happens, you do have a base framework with the systems you build, however when you insert your business process, it makes it your very own marketing machine that works for you. So, by simply documenting what you do right now? You actually reveal another section of your customer journey and the processes that happens at this time.

What's your current process, write it down

For most business owners, when I ask them what they do now, they point to their head and say, "It's all in here" or "We manage it on a spreadsheet" (what if you don't work well with a spreadsheet?) Even the conversation with the 7-figure business owner who managed to be generating lots of leads, making lots of sales. Yet the entire customer journey is in their head, so for anything to happen, it requires you!

Now that you know this, don't let this be you!

It's time to get this done, either you do it or you request it to be done for you. It can feel intense as you get pushed outside your comfort zone, however this is growth and growth is uncomfortable. I promise you; it'll be worth it as you'll feel the growth… climb the hill to the peak to be able to flow downstream with ease and grace!

> *To get results from a vegetable garden, you first have to prepare the bed, dig over the dirt, plant the seeds, water and nurture them… Until eventually they produce the end result! It takes time, so nurture your new leads, water them, let them grow.*

Another easy way to unpack your current customer journey is to document everything you do as you're doing it. Now this is a double effort, and this is what I did, it does take longer to complete the task. However, you're putting in the effort now for the rewards to come a little further on. Think— 'when I do this, I need to, when they do that',' I want them to…' it doesn't have to be perfect, however it does need to be done. Only if you want to save time, make money easier and scale your business.

Seeing this come to life for myself and for you, it's exciting for me. I'm the one who geeks out on systems, details and making it easier to do business online. And the more I do this, the more exciting it is to administer and market your business. It's easier and more comfortable to sell - because KP has your back. (KP is my Keap customer relationship management tool. It's like my personally trained piece of software to do as I want!)

Find out how you can get Keap at mates' rates with an exclusive book bonus not available anywhere else.

As an Australian Certified Partner, we get exclusive partner pricing and special deals. You can buy direct from Keap; however, it will cost you more. This is intentionally done by Keap as they love their Keap Partner community and they support small businesses to grow. Their partners are small businesses too: https://indemandboss.com/keap

What's a SOP?

It wasn't until I embraced understanding the sales pipeline that I really understood how having your business **S**tandard **O**perating **P**rocedures documented came into power.

First you need to know what you're doing, *then* you can delegate tasks to team members. If you already have all your workflow documented, it's even easier to come to someone like me who can take what you have and show you how to automate it, maintain the flow you want, while keeping it personable.

By creating documentation, you and your team can do exactly what you want to be done, the way you want it done - every time! You can even build this into tasks that include follow up call scripts, actions to take and more (you can really go deep on a customer journey and your own administrative tasks and client management). This is why I call it 'smart' because you look smart, and the end user has a beautiful experience with you.

It's time to educate, connect and engage to prepare your newly acquired lead to convert to a sale.

Start thinking like this…

'When a new lead clicks to download, I want them to get emails that educate them about a program I have that's relevant to the resource they accessed.'

Start with the end in mind, what outcome do you want, what is the end offer and what steps need to go between the opt into the closed sale.

Because the person has engaged with you, they are open to hearing more from you. They've given you permission to 'sell' to them - however, before you sell, this is a good time to educate them about you, who you are, the results you deliver and what they can expect from working with you or buying your product/services.

Think, how can you support them more here?

Educating leads is what comes next... getting them to engage with you (and take action) is the outcome you want them to do.

You can include frequently asked questions or should ask questions. Including social proof also helps build the relationship and trust. It's the phrase you've probably heard before 'Know, Like, Trust'

Help them get to know about you, so you can build on the relationship and build trust.

Remember the dating analogy, you're not going to ask them back to your room on the first date. First, you'll have a conversation and get to know them and them, you. Use this same process when connecting with your prospects.

A simple way to write emails that I mentioned previously, is using the copywriting formula P.A.S.P.A (Problem, Aggravate, Solve, Proof, Action) so you speak to the problem, aggravate the problem, then you're the solution, or your product/services is the solution... this lead is a hot lead and pre-disposed to buying from you. And you ask them to take action! Don't forget to include the call to action (CTA)

The slippery slide aka the sales pipeline

In your 'funnel' (aka customer journey) these prospects are now considered to be pre-sold on the services and you've pre-qualified them and pre-disposed them to doing business with you. This means you have delivered the freebie to them, and have asked them a question, got them to fill in a form or take the next action to bring them towards you (hence pre-qualified)

Do they click to open the email and download or access the freebie item (a smart CRM can track this link click and progress the contact forward in your sequence) When they do, you offer them a stronger CTA to book a call, go read a sales page, join a webinar or many other options here too, what you do depends on the journey you have for your leads coming into your business. Do you call them to say "Hi, checking in to answer any questions"

If you do any kind of follow up, that's good, it's a start. However, the majority of business owners and staff are flat out delivering to existing customers (I'll talk more on this in the next section as this is where you can save hours of administration and deliver a happy ending for your customers!)

When you're sending emails, think about how you can address any concerns they may have, be it an email series, a second resource, visit your website blog or view a video… What's relevant and helpful that you can share with your prospect to make a buying decision.

How can you offer more value as you educate potential clients? Showcase differences between your product and others, do you have any special offers, what else can you offer that has value.

What stops you from following up?

One last mention here is about you and potential fear about sending emails.

Are you one who says, I don't like to send too many emails? Do you feel you're sending emails that are not wanted?

It's a very common thought that marketing automation is impersonal, and that can be true. I've been on the receiving end of a piece of automation that screamed, I can't be bothered to do anything more for you here. It hurts and it puts me off wanting to do business with them, if they don't care about me now and they just want my money…

Do I want to engage with them further? My answer was NO!

Email marketing done right is permission-based marketing

Sending email from a smart CRM, or any mass email sending platform, they all have the SPAM CAN ACT requirement of 'unsubscribe' at the footer of every email that goes out from the system. It's not meant to be hidden away, and its actually good practice to do list cleaning and removing those who don't engage with your content. Sending to a dummy email address or spam traps will damage your sender reputation, and it's in your power to do something about it and ensure your database is clean.

The fear business owners like you may feel when sending emails to your contacts is real, I acknowledge it. I used to have that fear too. I've had that same fear in writing this book, however, if you chose to get the book, read the book and engage further,

that's awesome. I'm not sitting there forcing you, it's permission-based marketing and educating and building a relationship with your new list member matters.

The benefit of using a smart CRM is all emails have a quick and easy way for the subscriber to easily 'opt out' hopefully they don't mark you as spam, because they had requested to get on your list and you used permission-based marketing to communicate with them. And you ONLY sent them information they had requested!

If your system will allow you to do this neato little trick - what I call the 'kill switch'. It's a way of running an offer campaign and building an expression of interest list where you can send additional emails about a particular offer. Or, in your nurture emails you let them stop the communication of that particular topic. Some know this as an email preference centre and they're kinda the same. See the Campaign Examples chapter where the detail on this will be.

How do you go about going on a date with your new leads?

What can you do to improve it?

Whatever it is for you, write down what you want to have happen…

Now you've got an understanding on how to engage in a pleasant way, without neglect. You've been thinking about your sales conversion method and what you do now. It's time to put pen to paper and write that out.

Here's some additional prompting questions to get you started

- What questions do potential customers have before they buy from you?
- Have you answered these in the education/nurture emails following up the new lead?
- How can you address those concerns?
- Do you deliver more value in the email series, video series, additional white paper download or lead them to blogs on your website?
- How can you offer more value as you educate potential clients?
- What else can you offer as an additional resource?
- How can you showcase the differences between your product/service from others?
- Do you have a limited time offer?

Keep reading to dive into the offer!

CHAPTER 12
DO I HAVE A DEAL FOR YOU

> "I'll make him an offer he can't refuse."
> - Marlon Brando, *The Godfather*

While the line in the movie meant take it or die, your leads will get the offer and then move into the long-term nurture 'if' they don't buy! This is how they don't die and become a dead weight in your database!

The offer stage

How do you know if they're hot to buy or not?

If they're in the 'offer' part of your funnel, they've got here because they came looking wanting to buy or were open to buying now!

If you use Chet Holmes Buyers Pyramid, it's a tool you can use to work out the various categories and each category the 'buyer' meets a set of criteria. You can use these criteria in your marketing message to find the sweet spot.

The Chet Holmes® Method breaks down the entire audience of buyers in any market into 5 key categories:

1. Percent who are interested in buying "right now"
2. Percent who are "open to consider such a purchase"
3. The amount who are NOT thinking about it at this time
4. Those who don't "believe" they are interested (based on the info they have at hand)
5. Those who are definitely NOT interested

What category has opted in for your freebie/lead magnet/resource that got them into the top of your funnel?

It would be those interested to buy now and those open to consider the purchase. That's about 10% of the market.

> TIP: How you capture the other portion of the market is changing up your lead magnet, it's actually fascinating when you start to understand the buyer's psychology. And even more powerful when you can offer more to those not thinking about what you offer and those who don't believe they're interested… and you don't worry about the bottom 30% as they'll never budge from where they're at!

I've added a blog for you to read more, go to: https://indemandboss.com and search for Chet Holmes.

Let's consider that you're selling to those who want to buy (those in the top 3%) and those open to buying. It's now time to make your compelling offer. If they don't buy right away or within the first 30 days, then they've dropped down to the 'not thinking about it' stage and these ones you then put into

a re-engagement campaign (details in the campaign examples chapter) to get them to bubble up again into being open or wanting what is on offer.

Your lead magnet was attractive to your new lead. And as you've unpacked your lead magnet from your end product on offer, it's easier to now make the offer.

Knowing when to make the offer

Once again using a smart CRM, this piece becomes a lot easier as you've moved them along the buying journey from attracted, converted, consumed and now let me at it! So, after the new lead has consumed what they opted in for is the perfect time.

EXAMPLE: The lead opted in to get the free cheat sheet on 'the First 5 campaigns to automate and organise your business'.

Now look at the lead magnet and ask yourself...

- How long is the buying cycle, what education do they need?
- Does the resource lead them to further resources, a webinar, a masterclass, a sales conversation, or a sales page?

This is what you learn in your business services, and you will see patterns emerge and get to know what is hot and what is not!

If you've aligned with your audience correctly, they'll be going **"I need these campaigns"**. So, you make it easy for them to

get them with the offer. When they click to the sales page or whatever is the next step in your buyer's journey.

If they click but don't buy, in a smart CRM, a tag has been applied and they've moved along in the pipeline to get a call from you, and also into a new email series because now they're in the top 3% who want to buy. And if they still don't buy.

Forget about them… just kidding, there is still a chance!

They might have a few questions, so you offer them a call. If they take you up on it, on that call you make the offer and close the sale, or they may want a longer conversation.

Sometimes it's great to offer a short 10-minute chat and if they want to know more, they will then book in with you for a deep dive into how these campaigns would work for them. That's if this suits your business model. If your lead magnet is designed to go from opt into a call. This is what I call the Lead Magnet to Consult Funnel. (See the campaign chapter for more on this.)

The higher the price, the more love and attention is required

Generally, the higher the price point, typically there's a longer buying process and a few more steps to get all the details of what it means to them. Making it easy for them to schedule a call with you or be educated and nurtured via email or additional resources makes it easier for all involved.

Remember, 80% of sales require 5 follow-up calls after the meeting. 44% of sales reps give up after 1 follow-up. What will you do?

Now you may be feeling this is overkill, too much, however this is done on studies of the buying journey for a customer. It's also adapted to your own business buying needs. Do they get it, consume it and services is done.

For example: You might offer a service that a person needs to clean up their yard with a skip bin. On your website you have a 'request a quote form.' This leads directly to a sales conversation and they'll either say yes, or if you don't respond soon enough, they will move on to another provider!

If you have an automated response, you get notified immediately to your phone and you can make the call as soon as they make contact. Do you think this person who is saying 'I'm ready to buy now' and in the top 3% of the buyer's pyramid will take you up on your offer? Yes! Most likely… as they've done their due diligence, found your website, checked it out and then said, 'Sell to me, I want what you have'.

In this skip bin example, you then want to call and close the sale and I'll go into that more in the next chapter 'cash or card'.

Now, as you've considered your customers buying journey, they've jumped onto the smooth slide, they're attracted to you, you've built the relationship and it's an exciting time to make an offer. Now, what if you've given them the opportunity to buy and they fall into 'not ready'… well, they drop into the long-term nurture.

The road is long, but the journey is worth it!

This means regular content to keep you top of mind and it's not the spammy centred emails full of graphics! They scream *BUY BUY BUY*… I'm talking about education emails that keep them informed and interested with the invitation to remove themselves if they are no longer interested. You want those people who either changed their mind or went elsewhere to opt out! So be brave and invite it at every stage.

This is when you've built your connection and relationship with your new subscriber, what do you want them to do from here.

They've reached this point in your funnel, by going through a series of steps, these steps lead them towards you, your offer, so now is the time to offer. If you jump out of the gate when they first hand over their personal details, it's a bit premature as these leads may not yet be ready to buy. It is like asking them to marry you the moment you meet them. You will have them running for the hills because they are just not ready for that kind of commitment and thinking you are strange for asking for it.

Another thing this does is gives them so much value that at some point they will want to repay you for all you have given them. They know you are true to your word and are the go-to person that they want to work with so parting with their money is a no brainer.

Let's discuss the 'ready to buy stage' of your prospect

Think for a moment what it's like for you when you go to buy something. What is your behaviour…are you ready immediately? If you know what you want and are ready to buy,

this means you've usually done some searching and have made a buying decision, you head on over to the website and you buy.

This means you're in the top 3% of the market ready to buy, this is a very small focus group and if this is all you focus on, then you will be making sales, however you've missed out on a big pool of potential sales.

This is where the engage phase and the offer phase can work together, one flows onto the next and then the next through all the 9 stages we have here in these chapters and in the companion workbook for you to access and use to support you to document and create your 'sales pipeline'

If you can have a sales process in place that meets each buyer where they're at, you will tap into 6-7% of the market who are open to buying, not really thinking about it and even those who don't think they're interested to buy just yet, but maybe in the future.

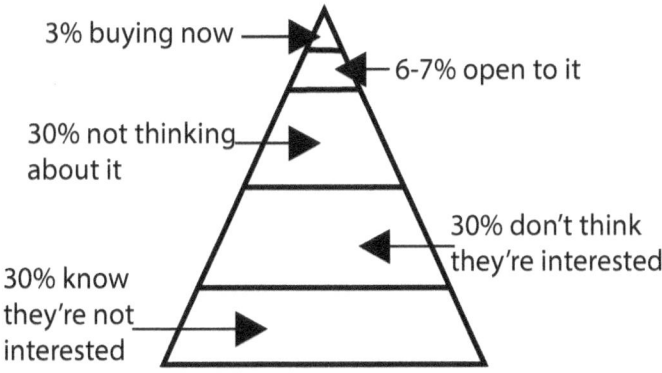

An example here is a webform for a real estate agent. On your webform you're offering them to join your 'hot listings' list where you send out emails to notify them of houses available right now. Who would be interested in this?

You guessed it!

The top 3%.

There are also the ones ready to buy in 3-6 months, and so on. If you try and sell to one who is not ready to buy for 6 months, do you think they will want frequent emails about buying now, or would they be more suited to getting emails that can help them prepare for when they're ready?

If you can find out where their interest is and speak to them and support them to move from not being ready to buy, up into buyer ready, it's kind of obvious that the sale is much easier, as you're selling to a prospective buyer that's qualified and has said I'm ready, sell to me! So, you move them into your frequent updates nurture sequence (using automation of course).

Final Thoughts

- It's not uncommon to lose leads because of delays in follow up. If you want to make sales, ensure you have automated follow up or a process that enables you to act **fast**!
- Check in with your emails after the offer has been looked at and they haven't purchased. These ones are getting colder so you can call them and see if you can convert them by answering any questions. If they don't want to take your call, drop them into the long-term nurture series

- Have consistent educational conversations with your leads and create compelling offers that entice them to move forward
- Be consistent and timely. Educate with an intentional sales process

CHAPTER 13
CASH OR CARD?

The Sales Funnel (Customer Journey): Closing the Sale

A very important question to consider:

Is it easy for your customers to give you money?

Whether you're making a new sale or a repeat sale, it needs to be easy for you and for the end user!

Whatever your means of selling here, either direct to a landing page that includes a checkout form, or sales call conversation or even directly in the email for the super ready to buy leads. It's much easier to sell to those predisposed to buying, they're hot, hungry leads who're active in your e-marketing funnel and your building momentum to entice them to take action.

Does it require you or your team to call and have a conversation. As mentioned in the previous chapter, a short 10-minute chat may be less imposing than a 60 minute discovery call. Have a quick chat first, see if this is a prospect you'd like to have as a customer, or if you need to recommend them to go a different route. This conversation can also happen in messenger, and you can filter them through to a free or paid consultation. If they're hot and ready, they pay for your time if it's of benefit to them.

The Sales Process

A well planned, documented sales process often uncovers more opportunities and will support in the close of the sale.

If you have a form on the website, when that form is filled in, you want the lead to bubble up in your sales pipeline and have a task allocated to a team member to call them and book them in for a longer call.

We mentioned in the previous chapter the request a quote, call, then next phase is the book a job. In some businesses the sales process is short and sharp. So having an easy way to manage this keeps everyone happy.

Taking swift action here is important as the lead is hot and getting colder each day, each week and will either buy from you or someone else who is marketing to them more frequently and consistently than you are. Will you do it the smart way?

Think about a time when you were completely sold on something. You saw the pitch, knew you had to have it, you were like, "Shut up and take my money!", only to face some hurdles. They didn't accept a form of payment you felt comfortable with, their sales page had too many upsells or there was just some technical glitch. Unless you *really* wanted it, you would talk yourself out of the sale and move onto something else. It happens all the time. Ask any business owner about their abandoned cart rates.

Do you want to have the B.O.S.S. time freedom method working for you and supporting you to scale and grow—in other words, closing more sales/getting more conversions without more effort?

During the M.A.P. calls, you get walked through a series of questions and one question I ask is, do you know your numbers? The idea here is to create a snapshot of where you're at right now, and what you know right now. This gives you a baseline of where you can make some changes and improve your results.

It's actually quite surprising how many don't know these numbers, and it's not something you focus heavily on in the earlier stages of your business. Money in the bank is usually a good sign the business is working, however knowing some key metrics will help you determine what marketing efforts deliver you the best results. Then you can do more of these things, it's always a test and measure requirement, because while you think you know your audience, it can change, and you need to adapt and change too.

This is where having some automation that tracks your prospect when they enter at the top of the funnel, and by the time they progress through your buyer's journey (which by now you're starting to see this a little bit clearer). Depending on the systems you use, you can get some really good data here.

For example, let's say you have an email nurturing sequence and you find that email #2 suddenly has a high unsubscribe rate and/or people just lose interest and don't open email #3. When you have a tool that tracks this, you can see where your marketing is letting you down and you can adjust email #2 to keep people sticking around for more vs losing people and having no idea why.

Now in reference to the smart CRM I choose and recommend, it has a sales pipeline, it's amazing and has made a big difference for all who go through the onboarding process with me, and they open up their mind to possibilities. Suddenly their sales

figures are sitting in front of them, either for them to manage or the sales rep.

> As a Keap Certified Partner, you get exclusive pricing and for my Australian customers, we get it in AUD. Plus you get an amazing onboarding experience and if you mention this book! There's a secret bonus for you too.

Go here: https://indemandboss.com/keap

Now, I used to be terrified of the sales pipeline, and I had very little understanding of what it was for, why it was needed or if it was relevant for small businesses. And wow…now, it's a completely different story and there's so much you can use it for.

The Keap Sales Pipeline

Because I use Keap for all my sales and marketing needs, I've no need for any other tool. And I learnt about sales pipelines and how amazing they are when Keap Pro made them visual, simple, drag and drop. You may have another system and you can apply this strategy with what tool you have too.

However, when you're not so 'sales focused' knowing and understanding this part and to become the 'salesperson' can be more challenging for some than others. Each to our own hey! However, now this piece is all visually available, the stages are automated, it's much easier to see where I have leads, who needs a call, who had a call and the project pipeline is awesome

as it takes care of the admin, reminds me to do tasks and nags me if I don't!

So, with the visual drag and drop sales process that tracks your leads, shows potential sales values, moves the prospect along the customer buying journey and much more. It's actually enjoyable to create some amazing sales processes that help you manage new leads to conversion, project pipelines, challenge pipelines, onboarding pipelines… you think it and create it! It's yours to be how you want it to be.

TIP: You can visit the website to read more on this as its technology and technology changes, so for me to say, this is how it is… well, it may not be that now. And a website article can be kept current.

Visit https://indemandboss.com

Other things I love about the Keap sales pipeline in particular

- Manually tracking leads yourself doesn't trigger any automation
- You can add in some easy automations— when you move the contact along (deal card) it triggers an action you have configured
- You can add in some advanced automations that add in additional functionality
- It's all in one system
- It adds up the value of all in that stage

When I'm providing the onboarding calls and training around the sales phase of the customer journey, what I want to know is:

1. What are your customer journey stages?
2. Do you have this process documented?
3. What is the next action you need to administer for this contact?
4. What happens?
5. What do you need to do?
6. Does a team need to do something?
7. Do you need to communicate with the prospect/client and when?

When you're new to a pipeline, this bit may feel irrelevant; however, if you dive in here and embrace this organisation tool, you'll know your numbers at a glance and be able to manage your leads like a boss. Plus, you'll feel amazing that you are rocking out your marketing admin stuff... go you!

It's great to start simple with no automation, just use the system to build out your process visually. This helps you develop the muscles to see where you can use a pipeline more, and little by little you can start to add in some automation.

Getting started with a sales pipeline

First, you work out what you want your sales pipelines to be.

We'll start with a basic service-based business sales pipeline.

> For the lead attraction [NEW LEAD] and you add the source and dollar value when this gets created, it will provide you a summary so at a glance you see how many new leads you have and the potential dollar value you could convert if you close the deal.

What's your next step, example [BOOKED CALL] if it's a sales call booking, then is there anything you need to do before the call.

When you do your call, you have four possible outcomes:

1. Yes! They're in and you need to send the invoice
2. No, not yet! These are interested, but not ready yet
3. No! Not interested in this thing but keep me on your list
4. STOP. Remove me from your list

When you move the contact into one of the pipeline stages, you can use the easy/advanced automations to do some administrative work for you. The beautiful thing about the automation is, when you set it up once, you can come back and tweak and refine which only improves it more and more. And when you first start out, you won't really be clear on this, unless SALES is your area of expertise, then you will be able to quickly and easily create yourself multiple pipelines. There's some analytics as well for reading the data of how long a lead has been sitting in a pipeline stage.

Now, I still consider myself a novice at pipelines, compared to a sales person who's been doing this for years! For me it's been a learned skill to develop the appreciation of the data, the management and the ease of flow when you start simple and go add in automation as needed.

I've built out a lead management pipeline for a franchise business that made it a lot easier for her to track leads and see where they were at.

The lead entered her CRM, the lead popped up in her Sales Pipeline and she was then given a task to call them. They also dropped into a follow up sequence and got an email, then on to get additional emails that educated them about the business opportunity they had enquired into. This being automated removes you as the bottleneck in your business stopping those ready to say yes taking action and it allows those not quite ready yet to get some additional information to help them make a buying decision.

Building out a full customer journey pipeline a few times, over and over during the onboarding calls, you see the benefits and how you can customise it to each business' needs.

There's a lot of power when you combine the sales pipeline, easy automation and advanced automation. It really is fully customisable; you just need to know what your steps are for each stage and what you want to have happen. Yes, this bit is related to Keap, however your system may have a similar setup.

Can I have multiple pipelines?

Yes! In Keap you can, and the stage moves can be automated. Start to see the customer journey of Attract to Capture (pipeline stage) through to sales conversation (said yes, said no) then closing the sale. SEND PROPOSAL/QUOTE/INVOICE (pipeline stage)

Another awesome use for the pipeline is THE PROJECT pipeline

When you sell a service that has some key stages and little things that need to happen at a certain point, you can have it setup

when you move in or out of a stage, automation happens… you put KP (*that's my lovename for my automation assistant*) to work for you. Time saved and follow up done! Plus, at a glance you know exactly how many are at what stage and you can manage the lead generation phase to bring in new leads when you're ready to close more sales.

You create yourself a slick Sales Pipeline and then you move the contact through to the Project Pipeline.

There's a lot more I could write here, however I just wanted to give you an insight into some of the conversation that goes on during the training calls and what I'm more than happy to share with you.

> Visit the website and you'll find the form to ask a question: https://indemandboss.com

In the selling phase of your customer's journey, you want it to be easy to get paid, either with or without your input. You want to be able to track your leads through your sales pipeline to move them over to your project pipeline. Get your workbook out and map out what your process is.

One more example is a lead to webinar to purchase a product workflow

The prospect registers for a webinar and gets a confirmation email and reminder emails of when, where, and a few additional pieces of information that will benefit them to show up. These are stick emails, which help your show up rates.

Do they attend, yes or no?

If they attend, they move into a post webinar follow up with the sales offer, give them the replay to watch with a link to buy. The emails also offer information to support the buying decision and a link to click to buy… then if they buy, they move over to the post purchase follow up piece (more on that in the next chapter)

If they don't attend, what then?

Is this a lost lead, lost sale? Perhaps…

What you can do is offer the replay, give it to them and also have the offer to click to buy a low price point product or service that solves the problem you addressed on the webinar.

If they don't buy, they continue on into a long-term nurture campaign that keeps you top of mind for as long as what you offer interests them. And they can opt out at any time too.

The point here is you've made it easy for them whatever path they take, it's the choose your own adventure pathway and this is where automation supports you to create different flows that you want them to go on, and they choose what suits them with what you have provided.

In this section we've touched on how to engage with your prospects to know when to make the offer and having a clearly defined process to close a sale while making it easy for the end user to give you money… you can access additional resources on the website: https://indemandboss.com

Some additional food for thought about converting leads...

- How do customers buy from me? (online, in person, sales team)
- Is this an easy way for them to buy? (Think smooth slide)
- How can I make it even easier? (Refine and tweak always)
- What are the top 2-3 things I can do to improve my selling system?
- The ideal outcome is achieved by having your sales process clearly defined
- What is your customer journey like when they go to purchase your service?
- You want to be able to consistently convert leads by following up
- Having a strategic approach with personalised sales process that utilises offers that solve the problems your prospects have to close deals
- Regularly engage with those who might not be ready to do business today so the business can stay top of mind
- Existing customer nurture content, to continue to build the relationship, offer additional services and create brand ambassadors

"Do not let any obstacles stop you. Where there are obstacles, there are also great opportunities."
- Dottie Herman

SECTION 4

DELIVER A HAPPY ENDING

> "In every success story, you will find someone
> who has made a courageous decision"
> - Peter F. Drucker

You made a sale. Now it's time to deliver and grow your community!

The goal of this section and all 3 chapters here is that you have an automated method to ensure your services are delivered seamlessly and without friction. It's time to deliver a happy ending! Woohoo! And of course, I'm referring to what is called the 'post purchase follow up' as the first step in this journey!

To ensure a pleasurable buying experience, you deliberately go the extra mile to provide an exceptional customer experience and follow up to offer incentives for feedback, reviews and referrals.

Creating Brand Ambassadors

If you can relate to any of these statements, you need to read this chapter!

1. My post purchase follow up is all manual
2. I wish my customers would stick around longer and buy again
3. My customers don't refer their friends
4. I don't do anything to delight customers

CHAPTER 14
DELIVER ON YOUR PROMISE

What is the purpose of a sale in business? To make money, right? Yes, but it's more than just that.

That's the basic fundamental piece: if you have no sales, then you don't have a business to operate. How can you ensure you make sales—and especially repeat sales— to grow your business?

Well, it's simple, really and obvious, right! Hmm… well, perhaps not to those not doing it!

I wonder… if it's that obvious what comes next and why do I see this piece as the biggest missing piece after a person has completed a purchase ie: post purchase follow up?

Even with a recent purchase experience, it was missing the follow up, the acknowledgement to say, congrats! You're in and we'll be sending you more information soon. So, I requested a full refund, it was only on the refund being processed that communication came to me! How odd! Trust broken and a lost sale.

You can't be around all of the time after a purchase is made, especially if you sell online. Using automation here is almost mandatory. Most tools will allow you to send some sort of follow up or purchase receipt.

Transactional emails are not true post purchase follow up though. That means, they need more than just a receipt or a delivery email.

Have a way to fire off some automation to ensure the new customer is welcomed and acknowledged. That they get what they paid for or at minimum an acknowledgement.

Why is it important to acknowledge a sale?

I'm surprised at how many times putting emphasis on follow up emails is needed. It's like we're scared to email people because we think they don't want it. If they don't want to hear from you, they will unsubscribe, but if they've just bought from you, they're expecting to hear from you. You want to let them know they've made a good decision with buying from you and you need to deliver the what's next in regard to the purchase.

This way, each person has had a touch point or two with you, each person has had an equal touch point connection with you. Each person feels valued. I mean, don't your early birds deserve a bit of recognition and a reward, should they wait until the same time as the last-minute planners, or would it be nicer to acknowledge and reward the ones who supported you ahead of the rest of the community?

I can tell you now, my own experience is you reward the early birds, and they will tweet about you a lot more than if you neglect them. You never know what 'story' plays out in their heads, that's not on you, however you can control the trigger for that experience, make it the experience you want… aka 'a happy ending'.

When using systems to automate your business, you want to ensure that at every touch point where they do something, you're acknowledging them. This is keeping it personable, not just a transaction. There's enough money grabbing Guru Experts on this planet doing transactional 'buy my stuff' crap... we don't need to add to this noise.

We want to create a delightful customer experience so when they reach the bottom of the slide, they land on a cloud, not a dirt pile that's a bit jarring and makes them screw up their face.

More than just a page...it's a marketing tool!

As mentioned earlier, the thankyou page on an opt-in form is often under-utilised. The same can go for a thank you page when a sale is made.

- Do you want to offer a limited time offer?
- Do you need them to book an appointment?
- Will you send them something?
- Do you need additional information from them?
- Is this where you get them access to your product in a member portal?
- Do you want to allow them to join an exclusive members only social group where you're building your community?

On the thank you page, it's important to give the 'what's next' steps and also direct them back to their inbox so they can engage with your email. Ask them to, it's a 'tell' not a 'if you want', you need to create the connection so you can stay in touch, deliver some extra value (see more on that in the next chapter).

The first email after a transaction, besides the transactional invoice/receipt purchase receipt part. Is you sending an email to say:

"Hey, thanks so much for your purchase, here's what to expect next."

Think back to the delightful customer buying experience you had before…

How did you feel and what happened? Did it all happen too fast, too slow, were you neglected, was it too much… or was it just right!

Cha Ching…Now what?

Let's discuss the benefits of having a post purchase follow up automation in place.

Whether you have a product or a service, you will still have some action required.

Post purchase follow up can be as simple as sending one email to deliver on what was purchased. Imagine if it also delivers such a delightful experience that your community builds and grows and you become in demand for your services, that they become a brand ambassador for what your vision is.

You align and build a community who love what you do and they're excited when you bring out anything new, they're the first to buy, and usually by this point, the fancy sales page and complex funnels are not needed, because they're already sold on you and your products.

Now a post purchase follow up may mean you adding the person to your member portal, if you coach, consult or package your services, you'll need a member portal eventually.

The addition of a membership site/portal/hub and post purchase follow up

I've had experience in creating membership offerings. And I have my own membership areas in use as well. They're my training portal, I keep them simple as for me simple is better than complex. You want to make sure the delivery is a smooth transition from purchase through to follow up.

I do recommend the member area portion is a separate asset from your main website. The end user experience is tied into a happy ending. And when you go to ask for feedback, you want it to be positive right! So, you need to put thought into the delivery of a happy ending!

If you've already got a member portal, it would be awesome if you have one where the systems talk easily and you can create a full engagement loop, tied in with a project pipeline (can you see how each stage flows into the next creating the smooth customer journey down the slippery slide) You need them to complete a module, when they do, they get tagged in your smart CRM and the next phase happens - an email is sent to congratulate them and guide them towards their next step.

A Happy Ending—Testing the Delivery

Hayden had an idea; he was delivering a service one to one in his clinic. He wanted to test out a monthly subscription product and make this service a one to many (he'd already

completed some of my previous training where he learned super simple course creation, so it didn't take much to get this next one going). He planned it out best he could with what he could see he wanted to do, but technology is not his thing, health and wellness is. So together we created a plan and got busy putting the framework in place with what will happen after the purchase is made.

The post purchase delivery method!

This particular setup became a little bit fancy down the track; however it started out with what was known and then added to as more was revealed, the gaps were plugged and it's now a tweak and refinement to improve, but the bulk of the system and process is there.

Hayden worked out that once they have joined:

- He needs information from them
- He needs them to buy a particular product
- He needs them to fill in a form and send a notification to the team when they have completed an action.
- He wanted them to remain engaged in the process
- He wanted it to be easy for them to show up and be reminded about the group coaching calls
- He wanted it to be easy to send out the replay to a select group of people, ensuring it only went to the active financial members
- If they left the program it had to be easy to offboard them like it was easy to onboard them

The membership portal is a standalone cloud based software fully integrated with his smart CRM, so they easily talk to each other. You do need to be careful of website bloat if you add

a member area there. You're better off putting it on its own domain or using a cloud based system.

When you can easily integrate a member portal, you can have triggers setup that connect the two and keep the communication going. All emails that go out link directly to the member area and help keep the members engaged and active in the course. This helps keep down the cancellations and improves continuity.

The best thing is the automation manages a lot of the moving parts in the steps the members take, from engaging in emails with a link click, to completing a section in the members area which triggers further automation. It can boggle your brain, so this is where it's important to start with planning, mapping - even pen to paper and draw out what you do know, so you're clear.

Now you know about post purchase follow up. You can test a person out, do they do as they say. What's their setup like?

One thing I say to my clients is, my emails are a teaching example. Everything I do is what I teach. I walk my talk every day.

Monkey See, Monkey Do!

If you're interested in seeing what you could do that I do, when going through my funnel, observe beyond what you see, put on your X-ray glasses and look beyond, what is the marketing strategy (remember funnel hacking). You may not see it all, as I have what is called conditional logic follow up in place. But you'll get a general idea of the flow.

There are some baseline foundations every business needs, and this is outlined in this book, 3 main phases, within each phase are 3 stages (a total of 9 stages). You must include them in your customer journey. Only if you want to keep making money and have a business that can become your luxury ocean liner you love that works for you and doesn't keep you a slave to making it work for you.

What do you offer when your community reaches an end point with you? Do they reach an endpoint, or is your well of knowledge so deep, that your community will stay with you for as long as you provide a solution to continue to support their transformation. With automation, you can manage your contacts very easily.

That leads us into the next stage…

CHAPTER 15
GRATITUDE FOR THE CUSTOMER

Let's start with you. I'd like you to take a moment and remember a pleasurable buying experience. What brand has left such an impression on you that you will buy from them again without questions. What about the brand that left you feeling used and icky, my guess is you'd kind of be hesitant on buying from them again.

Some products are one off consumable pieces; however in a service based business that has services packaged into products, because you're a leader in your field, you're always sharpening your sword on the latest trends and taking from that what is relevant and aligns with what you offer. You'll always have more you can offer.

Which business do you want to be?

Memorable? Or nah, I won't go back?

Once my daughter made a purchase, she got confused by what the display said, and she went through and completed the purchase. When she left the shop, she realised her mistake and asked me what she should do. So back to the shop she went to explain her situation and how the purchase was not what she needed. They had just sold to her to make a sale and had not really asked what she needed.

This shop refused to support a 16-year-old who didn't have a lot of money, who was doing her best to 'do the right thing' and acquire the tools to support the trade she was studying. This shop took advantage of her! It was a very poor post purchase follow up experience. Do you think the credit note would be used at that shop, or had that shop just stolen from a 16-year-old? Not very impressive.

How to impress your customers

On reflection, that credit note could have been used for a friend to get some products, however the bad taste in the mouth was still fresh, the icky feeling of how this was handled was still there. That credit note never got used. This shop didn't have any kind of follow up in place either, and even though they knew they had a potential sale with my daughter, if she had been treated differently, this shop could have had the credit note spent plus more. If the experience was pleasurable, you'd be happy to go back and spend more, but on principle, this shop was never returned to and has become a talking point many times over on what not to do. They're not in business anymore either… I wonder why?

Now you know better, you can do what is required to ensure you deliver the happy ending for every customer that passes through your checkout forms. Deliver then impress to get a happy long-term customer.

No one is louder than an unhappy customer

Did you know that a happy customer will tell five people about a pleasurable buying experience, and that same person will tell 20 people or more about an unpleasant experience, especially if they feel they've been wronged?

You've probably seen the rants on social media; some go really hard and name and shame. We didn't do that; however, here we are, discussing that experience. Go to any thumbs up, thumbs down page and see how one unhappy customer can cause a domino effect that can sink a business.

What could you do better?

Alright! Let's lift the energy here and bring us back to how we want our customer journey to be, how can you impress your new customer or a long-term customer. What simple offering can you produce that doesn't take a lot of your time, doesn't cost you a lot of money, yet it gifts the recipient joy, and leaves them feeling like a valued member of your community.

Yes, this is what you want, right?

You want to create a pleasurable experience, leave good feelings… that is why you're in business. I'm excited for you and it's my hope you will develop a pleasurable buying experience, deliver and as a result, leave a positive impression on your new customer.

Five positive referrals can bring in some good business; bad reviews can be very damaging to your business. I'll talk about reviews and feedback in the next chapter.

So, congratulations! You're now at the stage of creating your wow factor experience.

What's the next little thing you can do to pay it forward?

It's a great feeling to have connected and engaged to bring the prospect all the way through to a converted client. The smooth slide experience can happen.

What do you normally do now? Have you got it documented, what step do you normally have to do to deliver above and beyond on the service or product purchased?

Write it down. Each product you deliver on may have its own unique path; it may be similar or even the same. The minimum requirement here is some form of acknowledgement to the buyer.

If you have a 12-month program, you have the opportunity to impress the buyer again and again, developing a relationship beyond the purchase. In a coaching package, what does the next 3, 6, 12 months look like? Can you slot your new coaching client into a piece of automation you setup that has touch points and check ins, little notes of appreciation can go a long way…

Is there a warranty, or any maintenance on the purchase?

You can drop them into a follow up sequence here that's date timed and when a certain date is achieved, an email is sent, a task is created for follow up call or an action to be taken. This delivers additional value without more of your time.

You've made a sale; how can you impress them?

How can you deliver a delightful post purchase experience? Have you ever had an experience where you went 'wow' and

when you got the email to leave a review, did so without hesitation. Think back now to an undesirable situation, how did it leave you feeling? Did you feel valued as the end user? Do you want your customers to feel like a valued member of your community?

How do you want your customers to feel?

Create a way to stay in touch on a regular basis, have a way to ensure your customer feels valued, especially now they've handed you their money… they'll want to see some love from you.

It could be as simple as sending a thank you card, a handwritten note to say welcome to the community. You can do this as a manual process (and have automation remind you what to do, where to send it and when it's due) or you can use a service that sends cards with a printed personal message inside.

What you do here will be determined by the size of your audience. If you have thousands of customers, then you would need to automate it. What can you offer?

Turning $100 into $16,890 with a gift card

A colleague was filling up her car at a petrol station and she loved bulldogs and used to breed them. When paying for the petrol, she saw a gift card on the counter that had a picture of a bulldog. So, she grabbed 10 and wrote a note on each of them: 'Your next coffee is on me'. Aside from phone calls and text messages of thanks, three of the clients rang her with new projects that they wanted her to work on for them.

What cost $100 for the gift cards and stamps brought in $16,890. Not bad right?

Creating the WOW factor

What is it that you're doing to wow your clients and create raving fans?

What else can you do? There are many suggestions in the workbook for you to take and use as ideas and come up with your own method to deliver additional value.

Do you have completion certificates, some recognition of achievement can be worn like a badge of honour. I myself wear a few of these badges to support my brand and qualifications. These little milestones deserve acknowledgement, and it can be so simple, yet is often overlooked!

When you first start out automating your business, you don't start here with anything too much, you first ensure you deliver on your service and build the wow factor once the big chunk of your business systems are in place. It's important, however it's not a priority, if you have a really great delivery process, you'll be leaving good will with every touch point.

I'll share another example of good will, and how it's kept me a financial member for years and has me as a brand ambassador. All from a small bit of acknowledgement and recognition, I feel valued, and it keeps me hungry and wanting to stay within this community and give back. Remember I'm paying them, yet I'm happy to send referrals their way!

So who is this person?

Let me share a little story (and yes, this will loop back to relevance of the wow impress phase.

Back in 2015, I was a member of what was then Streetsmart Business School, they had regular business meetings we attended as a group, they held paid events that we attended as a group, so I was travelling a lot, studying a lot. One thing I did was go see a person to get some mentoring and advice. They pulled me up on what I was doing, why I was going to so many events, why I was doing all I was doing, he said stop it! Just do it! And I felt a bit deflated, I felt like I was doing all I needed to do and was filling in my knowledge gaps.

You see, those events were all with Streetsmart business school run by Mal Emery, one of Australia's marketing greats! These events got me up close and personal with some of the greatest marketing minds on the planet. Some I call distant mentors; some I paid well to be mentored by them. When I studied them, it wasn't only the content they created, it was them, how they went about everything they did online.

Influencers who have helped shape my marketing and sales growth were Dan Kennedy, Russell Brunson, Alex Mandossian, Armand Morin, Mal Emery, Ian Marsh, Glenn Twiddle, Pete Godfrey, Simon Bowen, Mari Smith Mari Smith, Jeff Walker, Ryan Leveque and many more... I also tapped into Frank Kern, observing him has taught me a lot!

There was also one thing they all did: they took inspired action, developed their business systems, and grew their team. They all had a customer relationship management system they used, and they sent out regular emails to follow up prospects, leads and customers to deliver. So, guess what I did for myself...

I took inspired action, I implemented business systems and I automated my follow up.

For me, I fell in love with marketing, I mean I'd started back on the web in 1996, so it was no surprise with the evolution of the internet and development of tools, that I would nerd out on systems and organisation.

One tool I loved and was introduced to in 2009 was Infusionsoft as it was called then. It's now rebranded to Keap and has three versions of the software so you can start out with the one that meets your needs. I used the tool and supported business owners for 5 years and was often asked if I wanted to become a partner… and it was when I watched a Frank Kern webinar where he sold done for you campaigns, I went YES!!! I want to be able to do that…

I completed the first of the online training to become a Keap Certified Partner in 2015 and I've not looked back. I paid the money, did the intensive training and became a Certified Partner, and it was during this time I met and joined Greg Jenkins of Monkeypod Marketing.

An example of the wow factor!

Greg runs a really awesome paid member group. And of course, as one of the top trainers on the automaton software, he has applied the strategy into his own business. One of these is the annual card I receive: the birthday card. It's a simple thing to do yet has a big impact and the feeling of recognition and acknowledgement that we as humans respond to in a good way.

So overall, the point of this stage is to have a way to wow your prospects and customers. By putting a repeatable, duplicatable

system in place, this becomes easier. It doesn't all happen at once; you get to this point in the priority pathway to success.

What will you do as a small token of appreciation to do for your customers. How will you leave a memorable impression on your customers, clients and prospects…

Up next, we work on how we can multiply and grow your business.

CHAPTER 16
SHOW ME THE STARS

How do you multiply your business?

Following on from post purchase follow up, there is a right time in your business to send out an email to your customer and ask for feedback.

This can be as simple as them clicking on an image. Visualise 3 emojis, one a happy face 😊, one a hmm okay face :-| and one sad face :(

Request Feedback and get a Google review
using automation makes this easy and time efficient

With one click you can send a customer three ways.

If they click the happy face, they go to a page to say thanks. On this page you can have a video message, and also verbally request them to leave a Google review.

If they click the hmmm okay face, they go to a form that has a box to write their feedback so you can get it resolved, make contact, rectify … whatever it is to once again ask them for feedback after a set period of time.

If they click the sad face, you get a task to call them and send them an email to say, we're sorry to hear you're not happy. One of the team will be calling you to see how we can rectify the situation. (Or something like that, whatever works for you.)

Throughout any of the above interactions, emails can be sent, tasks created, the customer record updated with the feedback provided. All automated and taking no more of your time, yet you get feedback to know you're on track or not and reviews from happy customers… which you then ask them to refer you.

What about referrals?

Is it easy for a happy customer to refer your business and get recognition for their efforts?

You can set up an auto-referral requester process. More time saving for you, and one you can control with the tick of a box.

When I start thinking about what is possible and the many various stages clients have engaged with my services over the years, I can reflect back and see the gaps, what was missing for me. And it is only in the writing of this book, did my own full customer journey become fully completed, only then did I understand the stage of my business and where my focus needs to be.

The flow goes from one, to the next, to the next

Creation of the smooth customer experience, from new lead to educational information and offers, closing the sale, delivering on the purchase, collecting feedback and then having your auto referral engine.

Another multiplication you want to have in your business is more sales. This is where you are sending your customers back through a new top of funnel offer. A way to capture their interest, a single click in an email. Or by creating a new landing page with the details of your offer. As they know you, and they're educated and nurtured by you. They actually like it when you come out with a new product or service they can tap into, because you've got them results up until this point, and done right, they are back for more.

How to multiply you in your business with repeat sales

A naturopath was feeling trapped and unable to do more. This 'laptop lifestyle' question was burning his ears. Working one to one with patients limits your earning capacity in a clinic.

Hayden took the step and started working with me, even though he was unsure of what he was going to offer to his clients as a course or membership offer.

As a naturopath he had so many different options, but he wanted to start with something that was really helpful for his clients, something that they asked a lot of the time, because having an online program as Hayden explains, "quite a profitable exercise because seeing five people at once is more or less what you're doing for an hour."

After completing the Wisdom2Wealth Easy Course Creation Method, in just over a fortnight, he had made an additional $6,250 for 5 hours work and was able to step outside of the office on the first holiday he'd been able to take in a long time!

Not only that, but he also now has a program that he can offer to either get new clients into the business or upsell existing ones and add real value to the work that he is doing with them.

Multiply by gaining feedback from your clients, build testimonials and reviews, case studies are a brilliant way to demonstrate your expertise and showcase some results. Your happy clients will be more than happy to support you.

Multiply by having ways to package your knowledge and create predictable streams of online income; I know it's possible.

It can be for you too.

What will you do as a small token of appreciation to do for your customers. How will you leave a memorable impression on your customers, clients and prospects.

In this section we've touched on how to deliver a happy ending with your post purchase follow up, ways you can impress and multiply your business. You can access additional resources on the website: https://indemandboss.com

Some additional food for thought about creating fans and brand ambassadors…

- What are five things you can do to add the 'wow factor' to deliver, impress and multiply your business to support growth in the first 30 days? For example: send cards, merchandise, coupons, a personal phone call of gratitude and appreciation
- What are five things you can do to continue to delight your customers after the first 30 days? For

example: surveys and check ins, birthday cards, holiday announcements and so on

The Lifecycle Marketing or Lifecycle Automation is a results-driven process

By having the three phases of collecting leads, converting clients and creating fans or brand ambassadors in play. By taking what you do now, plug it in to each of the 9 stages, you fill the gaps and then you have a smooth customer experience that will help you collect leads, convert clients and create fans.

The nine stages are way to view the collective sum of what makes up the customer journey for a business. If you use them to review your business, you can:

1. Gain clarity on what is working well and what isn't in your business
2. With clarity you can prioritise what matters and confidently ignore the things that don't as you optimise your return on investment
3. Confidence produces decisiveness which creates speed. Take an idea and quickly implement it to improve and grow your business

These nine stages form part of the foundation of the Business Operating Success Systems.

SECTION 5
BUT WAIT... THERE'S MORE

CHAPTER 17
THE KEEPER OF THE LIGHTHOUSE (LYNDI)

Who is Lyndi?

Technology is my comfy space and I'm good at what I do. For me it started back in 1996 when my daughter was born with Clicky Hips and I also inherited my parents old 486 computer. My parents ran a desktop publishing business from their lounge room, that same lounge is where I first registered my business name in2Web. I also had a nursing degree, and it was always a dream to be a midwife, that never came to be, so instead I took to birthing businesses online.

Back in 1996 when I first got started playing on the world wide web, I began creating little graphics that you could adopt; little did I know, this was just the beginning. Back then, before Facebook, there was ICQ Chat, and Dreambook, where you created a mini personal website and message board for yourself. I created a global chat room as I was stuck at home with a baby that needed extra medical care, so I couldn't get out like all the other mums could. I created a way to not be so alone. Mum2MomChat is where mums and moms around the globe came together. The dial up modem kept my landline blocked with a busy tone, but it was my escape, and I was able to help other mums and moms that were alone like me. I can still hear the dial up sound as I connected to the internet. It brings a smile to my face of where I started.

The first paid web job was maintenance of an online travel booking site. I can still remember getting a cheque in the mail for the few hours of work I'd done. It was good money to earn while working from my garage on the old 486 PC.

Life circumstances happened and I experienced children born with extra needs. I built a 6-bedroom mansion I wanted to be my forever home (eventually, I lost the house and all the proceeds to a con man! But that's a story for another day). I was the owner builder and it was a fun time, despite the not so happy ending!

Meeting bladder cancer in 2002, which was picked up during the 12-week ultrasound with my third child, tumours removed at 22 weeks pregnant and it returned again when my baby was 8 months old or so. I was diagnosed with chronic depression and put on medication. I had my first Reiki while pregnant and it fascinated me, so I completed my Reiki 1 and 2 training and enjoyed giving healings to a few close friends and myself. I also started crafting crystal gem trees and sold them—and I still do. I took painting classes and was commissioned to do a couple of paintings. That was pretty cool!

Life continued on for a while, where I started direct selling, then got into scrapbooking and ran retreats for women for four years. That was fun! I found myself back at the gym on a mission to feel better about who I was and took myself off the medication, it was rough! Yet I woke up and eventually the 14-year marriage ended badly and again, I was a broken woman, depressed and down on life.

My children are what kept me going and fuelled what little flame within I had burning. I had to change, I did want to find happiness again, to find me! I had to for them, I had to for me, and I did, slowly but surely… I can still hear my son saying

BUT WAIT… THERE'S MORE

"Mum, when will it get better?" Oh, how that broke my heart, yet it also spurred me on.

When I was re-establishing myself and my life after a big life transition, I decided to go back to building websites again and I also found myself at my first big seminar. It was a 3-day event in Melbourne and funny enough, was a seminar on 'How To Write A Bestseller', back then I nearly invested $25,000 for the experience. That book title was 'Food abuse and addictive personality' and that book is still inside me to this day, however, now I'm a published author in my own right, I've also co-authored Inspired Power back in 2018.

Anyway, I observed what they did at that seminar, the tech they used, everything, it re-ignited my passion. And now I still work mostly virtual, from the comfort of my home office with a global team and I've found joy through all the experiences.

Looking back, there was always an entrepreneurial spirit in me…

In primary school at what was called after school activities, the teacher had a room of noisy kids, some didn't have interest to be there, were acting up and affecting the experience of the other kids, so I got up and started helping the teacher, getting these noisy disruptive kids to actually enjoy the activity before them.

The free 'helping out', became a high school afternoon job where I went and helped the teacher out. I then moved away and that put an end to that job. However, it wasn't the end of my new found passion.

The passion to join a company started in primary school. I had found something I loved and was good at and could make

money from. I could support others when they were challenged and educate them on how to use the product.

At the age of 16, I was the youngest Hobbytex Sales consultant in Australia, this was a direct selling company of fabric paints, I didn't have a car licence and had to get driven to people's homes to make sales and attend the team meetings. It didn't stop me.

Which brings us back to the future… I mean present…

As I took control of my life again, the fun, loving, quirky character me started to appear again, I'm described as deeply loving and loyal. For years I've been working backstage in many businesses, building out the online footprint requirements, from websites, social media and it evolved into email marketing and business development using automation.

I've often been the one working behind the scenes to support the business owner. I love to shine the light on them, cause it's not about me. When I work with clients, I want everyone to see how amazing you are, how amazing your gifts are, how amazing your transformation is. If I can help you, you help five people and so on, then it just goes from there.

A thing to note: I tend to demonstrate a lot of what I talk about, I'm very visual in how I work, I like to see, I also like to hear, I like to experience first-hand to cement the learnings. I use the systems I train others in; I use the systems I recommend for others to use too. I never recommend a product or service I haven't used. (If I did, there would be a big disclaimer, but usually I would know the creator very well and trust them enough to recommend them.)

I do believe in walking your talk.

From Affiliate to Certified

These days, many of the tools we need to run an online business have Certified Partners, it's only from becoming one—after five years saying, "no… I don't need to do that". I truly understood what this extra step meant. The additional learning, the added value that brings, assurances for a level of knowledge, well that's how it is for me anyway. I pay for the best as I'm tired of being ripped off by well-meaning inexperienced, 'done it once and now I'm an expert' types. Though it can be hard to tell as a shiny front cover can blind you to what's really going on. Unless you can see through the facade, which I've learnt to do.

I needed this book to come to life, it's needed so I can share some foundational truths with you and if it speaks to you, we can chat and expand your ideas on the web too. I do things a little bit differently to the neurotypical mind, and it means you have a very holistic approach as you tap into all the skills, experience and life circumstances that have come before this point. My brain is my superpower and gaining unconscious competence is how I operate from the heart, it just flows.

Where there's a problem, the solution is also waiting

This is why I say, I'm Lyndi the keeper of the lighthouse, and you're the captain of your ship. I believe in taking 100% responsibility for your actions and choices in life. When you talk of the problems, I start seeing the solutions.

I believe you get out what you put in and I give my very best to all, because I know what it's like to be on the receiving end of some not so nice experiences.

Stay Healthy and Happy,
Lyndi

A final and powerful message, if you're ready to hear it

A giant ship's engine failed. The ship's owners tried one 'professional' after another but none of them could figure out how to fix the broken engine.

Then they brought in a man who had been fixing ships since he was young.

He carried a large bag of tools with him and when he arrived immediately went to work. He inspected the engine very carefully, top to bottom.

Two of the ship's owners were there watching this man, hoping he would know what to do. After looking things over, the old man reached into his bag and pulled out a small hammer. He gently tapped something. Instantly, the engine lurched into life. He carefully put his hammer away and the engine was fixed!!!

A week later, the owners received an invoice from the old man for $10,000.

What?! the owners exclaimed. "He hardly did anything!"

So, they wrote to the man; "Please send us an itemised invoice."

The man sent an invoice that read:

Tapping with a hammer........................ $2.00

Knowing where to tap.......................... $9,998.00

If a job can be done in 30 minutes, it's because there was 20 years or more learning how to do that in 30 minutes. You pay for the years, not the minutes.

Effort is important but experience and knowing where to direct that effort makes all the difference.

Note: If you're curious to find out what's available for you and if any of what we do here at in2Web Marketing meets your needs. I'll always start with a short 10-minute conversation: to schedule your call, visit https://indemandboss.com.

To work with us, you don't need to have anything as far as systems goes but you do need to be selling a product that delivers a transformative result. It would be awful for you to find out you could have saved a lot of money and time by having a quick chat with us first. We've heard it said many times…"I wish I'd found you sooner!"

CHAPTER 18
FREEDOM

WHAT'S NEXT?
What if you don't have any kind of system, and a lot of what I talked about went over your head?

Well, you my friend are in a very good position to transform your business in as little as 5 weeks! And you take this book, the workbook, put pen to paper and document your process. book in a M.A.P. planning session, get started on the 5-week business transformation training and join the monthly group coaching calls.

What if you have systems and want to do a check-up? I'd recommend an audit/review of what you have and ensure it matches your goals and what you want to build.

Having played actively in the world wide web since 1996, (Yes, I have been selling online since the dial up days) there's plenty of real time experience in a variety of the requirements for providing digital marketing solutions. It's a non-biased education review and recommendation session for you to take and do it yourself or plugin if needed.

The end of the day, the goal of this book and the B.O.S.S. method is to create better educated business owners who will adopt and understand their customers' journeys. It really is simple when you get it.

I love to create a happy ending for those who tap into the services we offer. You can also go to Google and look around… creating a digital footprint was intentional. I love the web and I'm into all things web… hence the name in2web holds meaning…

No more doing it the hard way. It's time for some simplicity, a deeper understanding and creating predictable streams of online income. Action what's on the pages ahead so you can do business the smarter, easier way using proven methods that are timeless and will grow with you as you need.

Get the concept, rinse and repeat = $'s in the bank.

To be successful, a business needs infrastructure

Take a physical shop front for example. You wouldn't question spending $40,000+ to do the fit out and get set up. It's obvious what you need to do. Signs, decor, point of sale system, stock. Plus, you'll need marketing to bring in customers. You then need to close the sale and of course, have a way to stay in touch so you can get them to come back and buy again.

Imagine you've moved from

OMG! I need to send that email, I need to follow up with Jane, I need to email Fred and get that call booked in (and the emails go back and forth to find a suitable time).

And when you think 'I want to run a weeklong intensive program that sells my prospects into my high ticket program', I need to create that thing… I want to run a challenge but how do I manage all the reminder emails for a big group at once!

BUT WAIT... THERE'S MORE

It's all too hard...

Jump forward to a future moment for you!

You have a way where the contact enters your smart CRM and from there it all runs on autopilot, yet it's personalised and sends them a personal message you wrote for them. They have a hard time determining the difference between you manually sending an email and it being fully automated.

It's where magic happens and it's about putting the 'care factor' into what you set up and knowing the customer journey or the lifecycle of the customer... where they start and where they finish only to be fed into what's next.

Imagine how good it would feel to open up your smart CRM and at a glance can see how many leads you have, what calls are booked, what tasks need attending... and you also know when someone pays you, they get added into your member portal and are supported to get whatever information they need prior to speaking with you...

Woohoo, congrats! Those notifications that say 'you got paid' are exciting!

They ('your perfect client') come predisposed to buy and love you for what you do. Their eyes are shining with hope as you've given them hope: hope for a better future, to feel better about themselves, because you made it easy for them to connect and do business with you.

I understand this feeling and it brings a smile to my lips as I remember hearing the words "It's working and now I can quit

my day job". When this happened for Sandy, it filled my heart with joy, it was a heart explosion of *YES! She gets it… finally!*

In Demand B.O.S.S. at Its Best

You will feel better about yourself, knowing you don't need to know it all, knowing you'll learn enough to not fear the business operation side of running a business and you'll feel amazing when you can go in and do something a bit techy because you've developed that muscle memory enough to know what to do with confidence.

A common response I hear is, "I wish I'd found you years ago." It's my strong belief, based on real time experience and observation, you can start this sooner than you think, small steps, one thing at a time, and soon enough you'll start to see the B.O.S.S. has your back.

Systems will set you free!

As I mentioned before, for many years now, I've been the 'hidden gem' hiding behind the scenes, eager to push the outgoing creative into the spotlight so it's easy for them to share their story. I say hidden, because as a 'completer' type person, I'm very happy tinkering away with the website, Facebook, e-marketing system… there's been many tools I've played with and learnt about over the years. Technology is my comfy space and I'm good at what I do.

Over the years I've developed my own unique skills having gained a lot of unconscious competence in areas I'm passionate about. This means I can see with X-ray vision into and beyond the front cover that's presented to me. I can feel the fear you

hold of doing this 'technology stuff', that it literally can drain your energy, because it's so out of flow for you.

In I come, all excited and raving about how amazing it is to do this. When I tune into your needs, I see it all forming and with your permission. It's created.

It's my goal to make this a fun experience for you, because it's fun for me. It can be for you to, even if you don't like tech!

I really love what I do, and I have fun doing it. I want you to have fun doing it too and get excited about the possibilities and what it will mean to you. I know this may take a little time, however when you experience what I'm talking about!

You'll go *arrrrrr* and I'll smile and do a happy minion dance—there's my happy ending!

But what if I already have systems, Lyndi?

You may have some systems in place, and that's okay; it demonstrates you're serious and have moved beyond a hobby business. We start with a review (diagnose and prescribe) and together we create your marketing action plan (M.A.P.) This gives you a clearly defined pathway forward for the coming months, a blueprint for your business, marketing, and sales.

You don't need the tool I use; however the tool I use by choice and preference has proven to be the best out of many and my decision comes from first-hand experience of working in many tools and having much frustration—and I'm pretty techy or have super tech on hand to help me decipher it!

When I decided to make my life easier and use what I call a smart CRM—smart because it does a lot for me, I considered it an additional team member who's got my back. I've said, please do this for me at that time and if the outcome isn't achieved, do that… it's pretty cool!

However, if you have a tool already and it works for you, great! You can take the teachings in this book and apply it to your system; the methodology and concepts are foundation building blocks for business and the tool just makes it simple for me to work with getting the desired results.

Ultimately, you love what you do, and are good at it, yet you know you need this 'marketing stuff' and it fills you with a heavy energy.

You may think, "I know I need to do this and I will…*later!*"

That's a huge mistake. Yes, there's an order of creation and it's not about going and spending 20 thousand dollars on a fancy website that you're not happy with that has static web forms that do very little to support you. That's a lot of money and it blows my mind to hear this from an exhausted, tired, and frustrated creatives who've thought they had made a good decision.

It's big ouchies and it's a big reason for this book… to reach more before they spend more than they need to on systems that set them up for failure. This book is going to set you up for success, if you follow the steps and put it into action.

It's hard to know what's right when there are so many options available, new ones are popping up all the time too with a special low, one time lifetime price! *Run away!* Yes, you need to stay current with technology; however, if you choose the

right technology, it will grow with you. You should be able to establish a solid foundation, have what you want, have it scale as you scale and most importantly.

If you take onboard what is said on these pages, if you truly become the captain of your ship.

You're going to be doing what most won't!

Congratulations! I'm thrilled to have you here and it's my hope you find this book edutaining, that's educational and entertaining. Simply reading this book and being open to the possibility of what's revealed and most importantly 'implementing' these proven business growth tactics… yay, you!

Visualise a cheering minion right now leaping for joy going, *yayyyy, yippee yahoo!*

Not only are you in the elite entrepreneurs' club, but you'll also get to establish solid business foundations to springboard off. You'll be gathering hot and hungry new leads. You'll have a way to get those hot leads to convert into hungry buyers to hand over their cash and then, when you deliver on your promise, your customers are thrilled, and you're rewarded with a growing community of raving fans who will spread the word for you.

We want you to embrace the methodology, rinse and repeat once you have actioned what's in these pages to stand up and be THE IN-DEMAND BOSS.

CHAPTER 19
CAMPAIGN EXAMPLES

Express Yourself

Did you know, in as little as 8 weeks, you can be saving yourself 1 day a week? It's not until you go through the process that you get it. Because we don't know what we don't know and you don't want to know the techie details, yet when the techie details gift you time… suddenly you have a new appreciation for technology. You're not the first and only one to tell me '*Urgh, tech stuff, I just zone out.*'

It's the real time experience for 20+ years that makes a difference. Working behind the curtain backstage with a lot of businesses from start-up to million-dollar turnover, you get to know what is needed (many whose owners left the corporate world to start their own businesses). They all needed a business, marketing and sales automation mentor, coach and trainer. They all needed a captain who wanted a smooth operating luxury liner. Together we went about setting up their business foundations using Business Operating Success Systems.

Together we go through a 'getting started' integration training then move into a deeper heart connection and then complete the imprint mark you wish to have on the web to scale and grow your business.

Appointment and Call Summary Notes

- After you've had a call with a prospect or client, it's handy to be able to fill in a form that merges in a customised note into a templated email that sends an email to the end user and also applies a date stamped note on the contact record for historical reference

Automation Marketing Website

- All forms on website are integrated into your smart CRM for automated followup, sales call followup and can also include tagging for list segmentation for personalised followup

Booking/Scheduling System

- Have a way for you or the end user to schedule calls in your calendar and send followup confirmation and reminder emails/text

Competition Campaign - trade show

- A great lead generation campaign where you validate their entry when they double opt in
- Once they've finished in the competition, you filter them into the long term nurture campaign to get permission before you continue to market to them (permission based marketing first)

Email preference centre

- Have a way for a contact to click and update what emails you send them

Event Followup on Autopilot

Webinar, Seminar, Training 1-1 or group, Live Events online and offline

- Have a way to gather interest for an upcoming event
- Have a way to convert interested prospects into paying customers
- Have a way to send automated event reminders and event details
- Have a way to gather feedback after the event to use as a testimonial

Lead Magnet to Consult Campaign

- The most common marketing automation.
- A landing page with a form that delivers a freebie offer that is considered to be of value by the end user, you deliver the item and include followup emails that contain a link to schedule a call. You can do a lot with this campaign

Networking - nice to meet you

- A way to add a new lead into your CRM and send a followup email to begin the connection, share information and find out how you can offer more

Newsletter campaign - long term nurture content

- Daily, weekly, monthly - regular and consistent updates sent out to your database, can be segments of the database to get a specific email. Kill switch used to allow the end user to stop the newsletter style updates. Includes a welcome the newsletter email sequence.
- We don't call it a newsletter, just used here for common understanding and reference

Re-engagement Campaign

- A short series of emails sent to a prospect or customer that's not opened an email for more than 90 days. Find out if they still want to get your emails and invite them to unsubscribe

Top 3 Needs Campaign

- Use this to build a list of FAQ questions and feed them back in your long term nurture. You link to a form that collects the top 3 needs, it can be incorporated into a pre call questionnaire.

Website Contact Us Form

- Add the contact directly into your CRM, followup, segment and create a task for team to followup. Send additional information based on option selections you've used to segment the contact.

BUT WAIT… THERE'S MORE

This is just some examples of what you can do

VISIT THE WEBSITE FOR MORE DETAILS AND RESOURCES
https://indemandboss.com/

WHAT'S THAT MEAN? CHAPTER TERMINOLOGY

The 'Geek Speak' Breakdown

Marketing and automation and all those words, what do they mean? Here's a little helper to give you understanding of what it means in this book.

5 Fundamental Campaigns

These are the first five campaigns every business owner needs. You can read more about these on https://indemandboss.com

The FIRST FIVE FOUNDATION CAMPAIGNS you need to consider are:

1. Short Term Opt-In Educational - Prospect
2. Long Term Educational - Prospect
3. Short Term 'I Love You' Campaign – New Customer
4. Long Term Upsell - Cross Sell Campaign – New Customer
5. Referral Campaign – Customer

Attraction Marketing

A strategy where businesses focus on showing customers how good the product is without telling them to buy. It makes the

product or service so desirable the customer just has to have it without any hard sell tactics being used.

Call to Action

Something such as a speech, piece of writing, or act that asks or encourages people to take action about a problem. Things like "Click Here", "Sign Up Now", "Add to Cart" are all examples of CTAs. You're telling them to take a specific action.

Content Creation Strategy

A systematic strategy of creating informational, entertaining or monetising content that appeals to your target audience to create and nurture the relationship from first meeting, to sale, to forever customer. It's able to be repurposed across all your online platforms, website, social channels etc and you can map out your weekly emails using this strategy too.

Form

A form also known as a subscription form, is a piece of code placed on any page of a website or blog where the users can fill in the fields with their data to receive emails, content or follow up calls based on what you are offering. The primary purpose of the form is opting-in subscribers to your mailing list. Though we never asked them to subscribe or submit to us! You gotta make it sexier and like a smart choice Yes! I want the Top 5 Campaigns Every Business Owner needs for example… you say Yes! Because that validates they're making a choice, they're in control!

Funnel

Just like a regular funnel, a marketing funnel filters through a large number of prospects down to the ones who are qualified and highly motivated to buy. It is a series of stages to guide prospects through the customer journey.

Indoctrination Series

It's where you share more about services, results or case studies and you share about your business and how it can help them.

You then move them through to a long-term nurture campaign that you deliver value to support them.

Keap

Keap (formerly Infusionsoft) is a private company that offers an e-mail marketing and sales platform for small businesses, including products to manage customers, customer relationship management, marketing, and e-commerce. It is based in Chandler, Arizona https://indemandboss.com/keap for exclusive pricing and a bonus offer as a reader of this book.

Lead Magnet

A lead magnet is a marketing tool that is used to attract people into your marketing funnel. It is a way for you to give value up front in exchange for permission to contact the prospective customer/client and start building a relationship with them.

Life Cycle Automation

Lifecycle Automation is a simple framework that small businesses can use to attract customers, grow sales and deliver an experience that wows customers. Lifecycle Automation was developed by a team of sales and marketing experts at Keap and has helped thousands of small businesses achieve success.

Lumpy Mail

"Lumpy" is the term used anytime mail contains an object that makes it stand out from a flat letter, flyer, or postcard. While a box could be considered lumpy, this refers more to packages that would normally be flat in appearance but are oddly shaped due to their contents.

Opt-In

This happens when someone fills out a form of a website giving consent to the business owner to contact them via email, text message or phone. It also shares their given personal information with them.

PASPA – Copy Formula

Problem, Aggravate, Solve, Proof, Action: you speak to the problem, aggravate the problem, then you provide the solution and have a call to action eg: find out more here, book a call, download here.

Results-Driven Process

Using Keaps lifecycle automation, customer journey 3 phases and 9 stages. It reveals what works and what doesn't. Thus, you get to create your very own results-driven process through each stage.

Stick Emails

When a person registers for an event, be it a webinar, free or paid event, online training etc. You'll want to have a series of reminder emails. In these emails you can educate about the upcoming event, you can seed information so when they arrive at the event, they're predisposed to buy or get more out of the event. You can use these emails to deliver additional resources and help reduce cancellations and no shows. These are an important piece for event follow up and can simply be timed reminders with a zoom meeting link. You want to make it easy for them to show up without having to hunt down your link!

Thank You Page

The most neglected page by the majority of business owners, because they're not marketers and don't know any better. This page is where you can inform the contact of their next steps, e.g.: go to your inbox and look for an email from name@domain.com Or you can offer an appointment, provide details on the purchase and how to access it.

Any landing page or form will have a thankyou page and it can be part of it or redirected to your website on a hidden page. This is the page people are directed to if they a) buy from you, b) opt-in to your form. This page can be used to offer an upsell,

encourage them to follow up on social media or to take the next step in their customer journey.

Tracking Pixels

Marketing pixels, aka tracking pixels, are essentially these tiny snippets of code that allow you to gather information about visitors on a website. Basically, it is the technology that allows Google or Facebook to follow you around the web and show you ads for something you may have searched for or considered buying.

Top Of Your Funnel

This is the place where your prospects start their purchase journey with you. It is where the most people enter the funnel before being filtered out. It is the place where you start a relationship with them.

White Paper

An informational document used by a business to educate or entertain the target audience. It can be in the form of an eBook or a simple PDF with the relevant information to solve the problem the prospect opted in for.

RESOURCES

Content Creation Strategy
A simple and effective way to create content for your emails
Start with the 9 blogs and expand out from there

Marketing Action Plan
Get your downloadable workbook on the website to complete and find your gaps

The First 5 Campaigns to automate
Where do you start?
There are 5 core foundational campaigns every business must have
What are they for you

see website for full details https://indemandboss.com/

ACKNOWLEDGEMENTS

To my best friend and companion David - Hey You! Thank you for all you do, I acknowledge you.

To Rod Cuffe - my business mentor and spirit mentor, deep gratitude for the support over the past years to reach this point in my life.

To my parents John and Patricia MacRae - who've empowered me to be the best I could be, always. Thank you! I love you ♥

To my 105 year old Grandmother Katie MacRae - an inspiration to many and a reminder to 'stress less and eat healthy'

To my brother Andrew and Sister Joanne - you always keep me true

A shout out to my Keap family who've shown me, and continue to show me the way with business automation, a special mention to Greg Jenkins, Jeremiah Sarkett, Chuck Hilbran.

And a special thank you to Clate Mask Keap CEO and Co-Founder and Scott Martineau Co Founder of Keap for enabling me to rebuild my life with passion and purpose.

To Sandy B - thank you for persisting and sticking with me all these years. It flows both ways.

To Dave Thompson and Davina Davidson and the team at Inspirational Book Writers for supporting me through this

transformational experience - YAY! I did it... woooahhh yes! Write on!

To Jean Sheehan for teaching me to 'trust it always works out', the Millenium Grid and Calendar has unblocked me and transformed how I do business. Thank you.

Gratitude and appreciation to my journey circle brothers and sisters who've inspired me in so many ways. Remember you are loved and completely loveable.

And to acknowledge myself, for overcoming fears, doubts, judgement, criticism and all the BS that's not true... the blah blah voice in the head didn't win! Joy prevails.

May your journey be filled with love and abundance always. From my heart to your heart, and the hearts of all beings.
Aho

NOTES

NOTES

NOTES

NOTES

NOTES

NOTES

NOTES

NOTES

NOTES

NOTES

www.ingramcontent.com/pod-product-compliance
Lightning Source LLC
Chambersburg PA
CBHW020643220526
45464CB00001B/277